KATE LARISCY

the house that broke me

a daughter's memoir of loving and losing through her mother's addiction

Copyright © 2025 by Kate Lariscy

All rights reserved. No part of this publication may be reproduced, stored or transmitted in any form or by any means, electronic, mechanical, photocopying, recording, scanning, or otherwise without written permission from the publisher. It is illegal to copy this book, post it to a website, or distribute it by any other means without permission.

First edition

This book was professionally typeset on Reedsy. Find out more at reedsy.com

Steven, Kinslee, Keaton, and Kole—
I hope to never leave you to grieve so endlessly in my absence or to wonder so desperately over my loss. I hope you always feel the love I have in my heart for each of you and that I never give you a reason to question it. You have given me so much to smile for in life.

Daddy –
All I've ever wanted is happiness for you. Thank you for continuing to give to us when you had nothing left in you to give. You are the strongest person I'll ever know. I love you.

Contents

Preface — iii
Acknowledgments — v
Introduction — 1

I   Part One

1. the green house — 15
2. ambien, my first core memory — 27
3. daddy — 34
4. the crack that crumbled the foundation — 41
5. a pepto bismol pink bedroom — 47
6. the red house — 55
7. first the faucet dripped, then the ceiling caved — 68
8. mostly storms, rare sun — 80
9. rehab — 87
10. the apartment — 99
11. the old schoolhouse — 113

II   Part Two

12. best all around & most likely to succeed — 127
13. my grandparents — 135
14. the house in tennessee — 145
15. the york street house — 153

III Part Three

16	a normal wednesday	167
17	tracy	172
18	a not so normal wednesday	188
19	the worst wednesday imaginable	192
20	madeline	200
21	the eulogy	206
22	the overflow drain	215
23	the toxicology report	223

IV Part Four

24	denial	227
25	anger	234
26	bargaining	238
27	depression	241
28	steven	252
29	acceptance	263

Preface

The intent and purpose of this book is to tell the true story of my life as the daughter of a mother who struggled for many years with prescription drug addiction. I want to share the hardships we went through as a family and how it impacted me through each stage of my adolescent life as I became more aware of her addiction. My intention all along, while writing this book, was to remain true to my heart and true to the story. There's intense vulnerability in opening up in this way—these are experiences and feelings I've hidden behind for many years. Which is why I've made a commitment to myself to keep it real and raw. I don't want to miss a single opportunity for someone else, who may relate to any part of this story, to feel less alone.

The prescription drug abuse epidemic is such an understated problem. I truly believe it's gotten to where it is because people are afraid to talk about their personal experiences with it. When no one talks about, no one is comfortable talking about it. When no one is comfortable talking about it, they opt to struggle in silence. They don't ask for help before it's too late. They don't recognize it in their loved ones or they choose to turn a blind eye because of discomfort.

My family was such a normal family. We had everything going for us. My mom had everything going for her. As an outsider, I would've never looked at our family and believed the hardships we were going through for so many years. I would've never believed that one person's battle could wreak so much havoc in the lives of her own spouse and children. I would've never comprehended the trauma evoked from losing a mother to prescription drug addiction after watching her somehow survive so many years of struggle.

If my story finds its way into the hands of just one person who needs to read it, who needs to hear that someone else has gone through or is going through a similar battle, I've accomplished what I was intending to accomplish here. If any part of my story resonates with someone else in any way, that will be more than I could ever hope to achieve here.

In this book, I talk about the reality of watching a parent struggle through prescription drug abuse and addiction. I talk about how interpretation and perception changes with time as the child gets older and becomes more aware of the truth. I talk about how age changes the dynamics of the relationship between the addict and their child. I talk about the sacrifices parents make to maintain peace and stability for their children. I talk about the severity of impact such trauma has on the lives of the addict's loved ones and the relationships it destroys in the process. I also talk about navigating the complexity of grief and finding eventual healing.

This entire piece of work has been my own. From the cover drawings to the edits to the publishing, I did it all. What you're holding in your hands is authentically *me*. So thank you for picking this up and for being here. I hope my story makes you feel *something*.

Acknowledgments

To my best friends and my first soulmates, Tracy, Alesia, and Sammi—

You held me up when I couldn't stand, listened when I had no words, and reminded me who I was when I forgot. You never gave up on me or our friendship despite every opportunity you had to walk away, every reason I gave you over and over again to just give up. You never did. When it didn't make sense to push anymore because all I did was pull away, you patiently stepped back and waited for me. You let me come back to you when I was ready, on my own time. Thank you for loving me through the darkest parts of my life, for being my secret keepers and my biggest cheerleaders, and for standing by me while I wrote through the pain.

This book wouldn't exist without your constant support, your belief in me, and the encouragement you gave me to speak the truth. You are my family, and you have been my light more times than you'll ever know.

I am endlessly grateful for each of you. This is as much yours as it is mine.

Introduction

My name is Kate and I'm the author of this book. It sounds kind of silly to call myself an author because all I'm really doing here is telling you my story. Nothing about this story has been exaggerated or made up to add fluff or to get a reaction. This story is just my life – exactly as it happened. The trickiest part of telling my own story in the form of a book has been figuring out the best way to put 30+ years of my life onto a few hundred pages. If you're reading this, consider that obstacle overcome. I found a way to do it! And even better, I found a way to get it into your hands. This is one of my life's biggest accomplishments!

The biggest challenge in writing this book has been finding balance. I don't want to share too little to leave questions or, even worse, cause confusion. Alternatively, I don't want to overshare and bore you with a book that you get five pages into before deciding you've had enough. The trickiest part of this whole process has been finding that perfect balance to stay true to myself and my story but to also stay true to you. Ultimately, this is for you.

I started writing this book in January of 2025. It was a decision I made at the end of 2024—that 2025 was going to be the year I shared my story. 2024 was a big year for me as well. It was the year I prioritized my health through clean eating and exercise. And I don't say "prioritized my health" lightly. I lost over 50 lbs in 2024 which is a lot on a 5' 3" frame. 2024 was probably the first time in my entire life that I've genuinely focused on prioritizing myself in all the best ways. Not the go get my nails done every Saturday me-time kind of way. Prioritizing myself in the ways I needed to because I want to be around for as much of my children's lives as possible.

At the start of the COVID pandemic, in January of 2020, I found out I was pregnant with our first child, our beautiful daughter, Kinslee. Going through my first pregnancy in such a scary, unusual and unknown time was hard to explain. We were afraid to leave our house for much of those nine months. It made for a very long, anxious period of time. But she finally blessed us with her presence in October 2020. Exactly 10 days after Kinslee's second birthday, I gave birth to our twin boys, Keaton and Kole. Yes, if you did the math, I can confirm what you're thinking—I was indeed nine months pregnant with twins before our daughter had even turned two. I still don't know what we were thinking with our timing on that. Though I do know we had not once thought twins were a possibility. It was a huge plot twist we never anticipated. When the boys were born, they weighed in total close to 14 lbs. I was GIGANTIC and I was also miserable. I was begging—and I mean BEGGING—the doctors to take them from me early. They wouldn't.

"There's nothing medically wrong with you. You're healthy. It's not medically necessary to take them early."

I disagreed. I was defying gravity with the circumference and weight of which my stomach protruded. The last time they measured my fundal height (which just gives them a general estimate of the size and growth of the fetus) at a routine checkup, I was measuring 56 weeks. This meant if a singleton pregnancy were to go to 56 weeks, that's the size they would expect them to be at. As a reminder, pregnancies typically last 40 weeks—56 weeks would be the equivalent of having a four month old baby in your belly.

All of that to say, I was huge. It was pure misery. I had also been diagnosed with gestational diabetes, sinus tachycardia (high resting heart rate), low iron, polyhydramnios (high fluid), among many other inconveniences. There appeared to be a lot wrong with me. But I was medically okay. Supposedly.

The point here is, from January 2020-October 2022, I experienced two full-term pregnancies and birthed three children. My body and my mind were beyond exhausted. They were depleted. Plus, my body didn't exactly bounce back after either of those pregnancies. In fact, it seems like the residuals simply compounded and left me in the ultimate state of self-image deprivation. I never felt pretty. I never felt good about myself. I never wanted to put on bathing suits or honestly even change out of over-sized t-shirts and leggings. My mental health was shit due to my lack of self-worth and severe postpartum depression. Everything was just in a really bad place. It turned out to be even worse than I thought it was while I was living it. I didn't realize how far down I had fallen until I was able to get myself into a really good place and could look back with a new perspective. I finally got tired of it—of feeling bad about myself all the time. So one day in late 2023, I got real with myself by admitting that the only person capable of changing me was *me*. 2024 was when I decided to change me.

Feeling accomplished and renewed at the end of 2024, I decided to set a new goal for myself in 2025. Sharing my story, specifically the part of it shared here in this book, is something I've been wanting to do for several years but have struggled with the vulnerability in opening up in this way. What I should know better than most by now is that life is too precious to be afraid to do something that has even a sliver of chance to help or change the life of someone else. So here we are.

As my daughter has gotten older, she's challenged me to face what I've always considered to be some of the hardest topics for me to talk openly about. She will ask me unintentionally deep questions at seemingly the most random times. There's never any rhyme or reason. No hidden agenda or ill intention. It's what four-year-olds do. They say exactly what they're thinking, often prompted by exactly what they're doing, at that very moment in time.

I know how their little minds work. They are innocent, naive, curious. They're unaware of the limited depth of their understanding so they search for answers to questions far beyond their years. For them, the world is a simple place. So they expect simple answers to the simple questions they ask us.

As with any thought and wonder a child at this age has, my daughter is trying her best to understand, to process, to remember every new experience, new face, new feeling, new idea. I try to remind myself of this when I begin to feel frustrated with our conversations. When I feel flustered and uneasy over the complexity of a topic she's attempting to understand. I remind myself that she's asking because she *doesn't* understanding and she's trusting in me to help her find her answers.

When I have these conversations with my daughter, I find myself envious of her oblivion. Envious of how naive children are. It's impossible for them to take things too seriously, to overthink, to stress, to hurt when their lens of focus is so new and untainted by the experiences of life like the rest of us.

INTRODUCTION

I often wonder if the world really is becoming a scarier place, the way it feels it is when you scroll through social media or watch the nightly news. More crime, more war, more hate. A whole lot less rallying together, acts of kindness, universal love. Sometimes I also wonder if it's possible it's always been this way. Could the reality be that all of these advances in technology and social media are now giving us more insight and awareness into all of the bad that's been happening around us all along? Maybe it's not so much technology being the driver of this. The news isn't *new.* We always had the nightly news playing in our living room while I was growing up. Maybe the real difference is that now I've been around long enough, grown old enough, to finally acknowledge and understand the truth and reality I was a stranger to as a child. When I think about it this way, it feels more likely that I am just finally seeing what was there all along.

It seems that, as children, our parents do their best to protect us from this scary world that surrounds us. The scary world they bring us into that they immediately feel responsible for protecting us from. They guard us by keeping us in our little bubble of childhood innocence for as long as they can. While we're in this bubble, they filter out as much of the bad stuff as they can so that most of what we see as children is the good. By doing this most, if not all, of what we know is the good in the world. They stay there—standing guard outside of our childhood bubble as our fearless protectors—for as long as they physically can. Until inevitably, they lose their power and desire to contain. They know they can't keep us in that bubble forever. It's not good for us and it's not good for them. They know that. So when they step aside, almost as soon as they do, the bubble of childhood innocence pops. The once child must now face the reality of the world as it's always been—except this time, it's on their own. For the first time, they are able to see what all they were sheltered from by their parents. The world as they see it looks a whole lot different now.

Some of the questions my daughter asks are relatively simple to answer.

"Why don't you and daddy work on Saturdays and Sundays?"
"Are unicorns real?"
"Why are there clouds in the sky?"
"Do we stop when the light is red?"

And then there are some that stump me. Questions that stop me in my tracks and leave me second guessing, long after they conversation has ended, if what I told her was too much or not enough. I wasn't anticipating her curiosity over things like this so early in life.

"Mommy, where did your mom go? How come I've never met her?"

"Did she go to heaven like Rocky?"

"But why did she go to heaven, Mommy? She didn't want to stay here with us?"

After careful consideration, I've decided to reply with honesty and ambiguity. Not to withhold from her but to protect her. She's still very much living in the bubble of childhood innocence after all.

"Yes, my mommy went to heaven just like Rocky. She's your angel and she loves you more than anything. She is watching over you."

My hope is that one day, when the time is right and her curious mind is old enough to better understand life and all of its complexities, she'll open this book and find all her answers. I don't want the answers she finds here to hurt her. I would never want her to hurt over this. My hope is that finding her answers will help her understand me better. My hope is that it makes sense of why she never had the opportunity to meet my mom, her grandmother. I want my daughter to know as much as she wants to know about the complicated life I lived before her existence. I want her to understand why she was never given the opportunity to meet her grandmother. I want her to know about the years of my life that gave me profound strength—strength that I hope will make her proud one day.

It's been 10 years since my mom lost her battle with prescription drug addiction. I've grieved deeply over the past decade and spent copious amounts of time living in each of its so-called *stages*. I've learned on my own time and in my own experiences that stages of grief aren't as simple or defined as they are made out to be when you read about them on paper. The five stages of grief seem pretty clear cut, right? Denial, anger, bargaining, depression, acceptance. My experience has not been what I would describe as clear cut. Grief is not that you sit in one stage and feel those feelings for a while before you naturally evolve to the feelings outlined in the next stage of grief and that process repeats until you've reached acceptance—when you have official permission to move on with your life. Grief is nothing like that. At least that's not been my experience with it. It's been cyclic, even disorderly at times, and it repeats itself over and over again.

What I've experienced in grief has felt unusual at times. I often wonder if others in similar shoes can relate to these feelings. There have been times in my life over the past 10 years that have been so joyful—so perfect—that I've briefly forgotten that I ever lost my mom. Almost as if she never existed in the first place so grieving is therefore a moot point.

It's like the only way I've been able to feel these intense feelings of such happiness and bliss is through logical separation from the huge void in my life. To forget that she left. To forget that she was ever here at all. To forget about her. All so that I can allow myself to feel joy.

It hurts my heart to say it but sometimes I fail to recall the idea of ever having a mom. As time passes by, the memory of her prior existence and what it felt like to have her here are intangible treasures that have slowly slipped away. The reality is, I've had no choice but to continue life without her. To adapt to her void. I've heard that if you do something consistently for long enough, it becomes habit. I guess I've developed a habit for being motherless. I wonder if this means I've finally reached *acceptance*. Sometimes this realization makes me proud of how far I've come. Sometimes it devastates me. Sometimes it shows itself in the form of anger and envy towards those that have never had to live a day of their lives without their mom. Sometimes I find myself wondering, why did this have to happen to me?

On the other side of being in this seeming stage of *acceptance*, there are moments I forget any of this ever happened. I'll get good news at work and instinctively pick up my phone to call her first. Does this put me back in *denial*? Sometimes I find myself in the middle of a mundane task, like washing the dishes, when I'm hit with the sting of the initial shock of her death all over again—out of nowhere. The pit in my stomach. The lump in my throat. Weakness in my knees as if they may just give out right there. All as if I've just been reminded of losing her. But my mind doesn't let me stay fooled for long—it quickly floods me with the haunting flashbacks to that terrible night. The night my mom died. The flashbacks in these moments fill me with overwhelming sadness—sadness for me but also sadness for her. I know how sad she would be over the life she left behind.

It still doesn't make sense to me, why this had to happen to *our* family. Why us? What did we do wrong to the universe to deserve this? It will probably never make sense because losing my mom at just 24-years-old myself really isn't something to make sense of.

Even if this story isn't one I'll ever be able to make sense of, it's one I want to share. It's a story I *need* to share for myself, for my family, and for anyone else who resonates with or is impacted by a similar story of their own.

Some time ago, I read an article about the science and psychology of memory—specifically, how our brains recall past experiences. It's a surprisingly complex process, far different from what I had imagined. I'm no expert, but I've come away with a basic understanding that I want to share with you. And yes, there is a point to all of this—I promise.

In simple terms, our brains don't record and store memories like video footage. We don't preserve an experience exactly as it happened, ready to be replayed later. If it were that straightforward, I wouldn't be bringing it up.

Instead, what we store are small visual fragments—like scattered photographs of individual moments. These fragments are kept throughout the brain, separate from the emotions or sensations we felt at the time. When we try to remember something, our minds piece those snapshots back together—like assembling an old jigsaw puzzle. And where pieces are missing, the brain fills in the gaps with what seems logical or familiar. The end result is the memory we "recall"—a reconstruction, not a replay.

This is really interesting to me because it helps explain why two people can have completely different memory of the same shared experience. The emotions piece is fascinating to me as well because it means that any feeling felt when a memory is recalled is not *the* feeling from the original experience itself. Your brain does not store the emotional response component of an experience. This means you are in complete control of how a memory from the past makes you feel. How a memory makes you feel is your current, real-time emotional response to the memory. It has nothing to do with what you were feeling when that experience was happening in real time. It really is fascinating.

Anyway, I say all of this not to start the book off with a lesson on the psychology and physiology of the human brain. I am sharing this because I feel it's important to understand how memories really work. Especially while writing a book based on 30+ years of memories. It has helped me make sense of how I've seemingly managed to store away so much detail from so many years of my life. I've always been able to recall very vivid memories of specific events surrounding my mom. I also have a general understanding of how the brain is constructing these memories. I know that not every little moment of the memory can be or is exactly as I experienced it.

My intention is to tell my story based on what I remember from my experiences with an addict mom. The easiest way for me to tell this story, this part of *my* story, is by starting where I feel it began and describing how I felt it evolved. I want you to see how things can go from bad to worse right before your eyes. I want to show you how two very different worlds can coexist in the world of addiction. Two very different people can coexist in one human body. Outside of those closest to me or my family at the time, I don't think many had even a clue as to what was going on in our lives. Even for those that knew *something*, it was so much more than they could've even imagined. So much more than anyone could've ever possibly understood unless they were going through it themselves.

I also want readers to know that, despite my mom struggling with addiction for many years, the other parts of my life prior to and during the worst of her battle were very normal. I think that's why many, at least those of you that know me, will find a lot of this story a bit surprising. Potentially even shocking at times. The normal parts of our lives were what those around us and even closest to us saw. At least for the most part—there may have been a few exceptions here or there. We went to church on Sundays. We spent weekends at Edisto beach with my mom's best friends from high school and their families. We saw movies at the local theater on Saturday nights like many other families around us. We did everything a normal family would do. What we had going on in our lives was the perfect example of "you really never know what someone is going through."

We spent just enough of my life in normalcy to allow me to look back on my childhood and feel overwhelming love and appreciation for my parents and the good parts of our upbringing. My mom was a great mom for many years. I never questioned her love for any of us. In fact, to this day, I still don't think I'll ever be loved the way she loved me again in this lifetime. I guess I spent enough time with her in my life, without pills, to be able to tell you about all of her mistakes and struggles, about all the ways she hurt me and broke me, about all the years I've spent picking up the pieces from the life she shattered and still be able to say that my mom was a good mom and without a shadow of a doubt one of the best humans I'll ever know. It goes to show that bad things happen to good people. Addiction is a terrible, terrible thing.

Whether or not this story resonates with you, I hope it invites reflection. I hope you find it perplexing and enlightening, disappointing and rewarding, challenging and encouraging—a complex blend of contradictions, much like life itself, much like loving an addict. Above all, may it remind you that sometimes we must break before we can begin to heal—that even the deepest cracks in a broken foundation can become the very places where growth takes root, often in the most unexpected ways.

Author's Note:

For the privacy and protection of certain individuals, some names and identifying details have been changed. While the events and emotions portrayed are true to the author's memory and experience, select identities have been altered to respect the confidentiality of those involved.

Part One

2002-2008

1

the green house

2002-2004

We were a family of movers, the four of us—my mom, dad, sister, and me. Actually, it was probably safe to say that we were borderline gypsies with our unexplained nomadic lifestyle. We moved constantly and for no apparent reason. At least that's how it seemed to me for many years. To me, it seemed like my parents just liked to move around. They liked to live in different types of houses where they could dabble with new styles and overcome uncharted challenge in the form of house projects. Most of the time I didn't mind moving around. Not that minding it would've changed anything. I was just along for the ride. There were certainly positives to changing things up every now and then. When I got old enough to have a descent sense of style and taste, my parents were pretty open to the idea of my having a say in the theme and paint color for each of my new bedrooms.

In one house, I chose an *African theme*—complete with safari green leopard sheets, a premium down comforter in zebra print, and a rain stick that served no purpose other than sitting propped up in the corner of my room to show off to infrequent visitors. In another house, I had what my parents called *Pepto Bismol pink* walls to match the accents of my custom-designed draperies and Pottery Barn duvet with matching shams. My sister and I never had to take part in any of what most would see as burdens of moving houses—the packing and unpacking, keeping the listed house in pristine condition in case of any last minute showings, negotiating with potential buyers. So for me, it was just a new house in a new neighborhood with a new bedroom that I got to pick out new stuff for. Not such a bad end of the deal if I say so myself.

Each house we lived in felt like a new and different chapter—similar to the structure of this book. Some chapters were happier, more normal and predictable than others. Some were filled entirely with misfortune, outcomes you'd never be able to fathom in another life. Regardless of the physical location of each house and what happened behind each of their doors, they all felt exactly like home to me. I guess it was the people that made the home, not the house itself.

It was normal to me for us to move around a lot. It's all I ever knew. It *was* our normal. I never experienced what I'd consider to be the normal for most. To grow up in one specific house. To stay in *my* bedroom, that one bedroom I always had, when visiting my parents in the house I grew up in years after I moved away. I can see the appeal of it for sure. The rush of nostalgia as soon as you walk in the door. Being instantly flooded with memories from the best 15+ years of your life. While I never had this luxury, that *one home,* my parents somehow made every house we lived in feel like we'd always been there. It could've been the furniture, the rugs, the curtains all being mostly the same. Maybe because all of our stuff traveled with us with each move, each new house still smelled like us. I don't know how they did it but no matter where we were, we were home.

My mom loved pleasant scents. 3-wick candles and wallflower plugins from Bath & Body Works were a staple in our houses. Much like the house I live in with my own family now, almost every room in the house had a wallflower plugged into an outlet. She was strategic with her scents though—she never wanted it to be overpowering or offensive to house guests. The scents she chose were clean and delicate. Our house always smelled fresh—but not the kind of fresh and clean like you just spent five hours cleaning every room from floor to ceiling before your guests arrive. Though she would go a little crazy with the chore list before hosting any events at our house. But this wasn't that kind of smell. It wasn't bleachy. It was just fresh. Kind of like walking into an Anthropologie store—if you've ever been inside one of those. So maybe there's my answer. Every house smelled and felt like it'd always been our home because the wallflowers traveled with us. Gotta love those wallflowers.

I was 12 years old in 2002–seventh grade. I had what my mom always called "dishwater blonde" hair at that age. It went from bright blonde as a toddler to medium brown as an adolescent to that lovely dishwater blonde color in my early teens. If you haven't heard of dishwater blonde, it's basically a dull blend of dark blonde and light brown. If it lives up to it's name, you should be able to get an idea of its shade by washing a load of dishes in the sink and peaking in at the dirty water when you're done. That color. If I didn't color my hair, it'd still be the same dishwater blonde that I see glimpses of when I wait too long between hair appointments.

I look back on pictures of myself at this age and feel like I just looked awkward. I can only hope I wasn't as awkward as I appeared in those pictures. This was the age I started over-plucking my beautifully full set of eyebrows because thin brows were "in" in the early 2000s. I hated my bushy eyebrows. One of my uncles told me one time, when I was a little younger than this, that my eyebrows looked like Brooke Shields'. I didn't know what that meant when he said it. He probably meant it as a compliment but I took it as the biggest insult. I hated my eyebrows. Ironically, people now pay to get those eyebrows tattooed onto their faces. Funny how time changes things. At this age, I was also big into tight jeans with no back pockets. Apparently no pockets made your butt look bigger and that's why all the girls liked wearing them. I was also starting to dabble with makeup at this age. My mom always loved makeup so I'm sure that part of this stage excited her. Someone to share her love of makeup with—finally. I guess I didn't appear to go heavy on the makeup though because in pictures you can barely see it— just a touch of mascara, pencil thin eyebrows, and tight jeans.

Leading up to official entry into my teenage years, I had always maintained a pretty thin physique. I attributed that mostly to the discipline and physicality of years of ballet. But as soon as I hit puberty nearing the end of seventh grade, my body shape began to change dramatically. For the first time in my life, I had curves. Seventh grade marked the beginning of both my teenage years and my journey into womanhood.

All I can think of when I think back to my experience in seventh grade is how mean middle school girls could be. I truly already dread these days for my own daughter. I can only hope it's gotten better since I went through it. I doubt it though—middle school girls are middle school girls. It really was that bad. It's hard to believe at just 12 years old, you can cry yourself to sleep at night over drama with your friends. Realistically, friends is a loose term at 12 years old—at least it was for me. If you have keeper friends at 12 years old, you should consider yourself a lucky individual. I can't pretend I was an angel myself. I was an equal contributor to the mean girl antics.

Some of the things we did to each other, said about each other, wished on each other were not things real friends would do. Which is exactly why we'd get into these huge fights with each other, not talk for a week, and then pretend like nothing ever happened. It was as if we simply got bored with being mad at each other so we just dropped it and were "best friends" again. It's so silly to think back on. But it didn't feel silly when I was in the thick of it. Pre-teen girls could be evil.

I remember one argument so vividly, even 20+ years later. I bought matching shirts with another girl in our friend group. The shirt had "Mistletoe Magnet" printed across the chest. So scandalous. In reality, I had never even kissed a boy. The shirt implied otherwise. But anyway, we bought these matching shirts with plans to wear them on an upcoming overnight school trip to Williamsburg, VA. For some reason this seemed like a good idea to us. Just thinking back to those shirts and wearing them at 12 years old makes me cringe. Adding that on top of wearing them on a chaperoned field trip makes me embarrassed for myself. But that's beside the point. When we got ready that first morning in the hotel room a few of us were sharing, the two of us excitedly put on our jeans and matching mistletoe shirts. When our other friend walked out of the bathroom and saw that we had coordinated outfits without her, she was furious. In her mind, we purposefully and cunningly excluded her from our matching shirt plans. After sharing a few words in the heat of the moment, she didn't talk to us for the rest of the school trip. It made our shared hotel room stay and bus seat assignment extremely awkward and uncomfortable. All because of those stupid mistletoe magnet shirts. Little did she know she looked the least foolish by not matching us that day.

That's what middle school girls did though. I'm sure they still do it. They argue over the dumbest things that seem so significant at 12-13 years old, they say the cruelest things to each other, and then they don't talk for several weeks. But then one day out of the blue, they wake up and decide they're no longer mad at each other and its never mentioned again. It's as if it never happened. Which is what happened after our Williamsburg trip. Just as predicted, within a few days of coming back from our trip, we were all best friends again. I'm also fairly certain we all went back to Target together to get her a matching mistletoe magnet shirt. Our unspoken agreement that we had all forgiven each other. This fighting and making up was also a very cyclic process. It's how I'd sum up my perception and memory of middle school.

At 12 years old, I was living the life of an "army brat". I think that's an appropriate way to describe my life at least—with the exception of neither parent being in the military. By 2002, our family of four had already lived in five different houses together, been residents of two different states (including several towns within each of those states) and ultimately landed back where we all started, in South Carolina. We'll get into more of that—the part about leaving and then coming back to South Carolina—later.

In 2002, we had just moved out of Aiken, South Carolina and were living in a newly built house in a new subdivision on the outskirts of Columbia, South Carolina. Technically a portion of the neighborhood was in Blythewood but the vast majority was in Columbia. I only know this because there were two high schools in the area - one more desirable than the other and those living on the Blythewood side of the neighborhood were, what I considered, the lucky ones. For what it's worth, we were *not* in the Blythewood section of the neighborhood but my parents worked with the school district to help get me into what would eventually become my preferred high school. There was nothing wrong with the high school I was zoned for by the way, I just wanted to stay with all my friends from middle school who were going to the high school I wasn't zoned for.

This new subdivision we found ourselves in in the early 2000s was called Lake Carolina. At the time, it was pretty isolated from other developments. Unfortunately, times have changed since then. This whole side of town is now, in my opinion, overcrowded. Most of the trees have been plowed down and the once two lane road has been expanded to four. But back then, its chosen location was perfectly isolated. Surrounded by nature and placed right beside the man-made lake that would eventually become its biggest selling point for prospective buyers.

I remember the day my parents visited Lake Carolina for the first time. We spent hours in their Welcome Center that day. It was a building just as extravagant as the water fountain that sat at the center of the neighborhood's entrance.

I say this and think about how funny it is to see things from a different perspective as you get older. Things that used to look "HUGE" really aren't so big when you get a chance to see the world that sits outside your childhood bubble. This shift in perspective happens to me a lot when I return to places as an adult that I haven't been since childhood.

The sales agent that met with us at the Welcome Center that day showed my parents future design plans for the community which promised schools, a gas station, restaurants, a grocery store, and movie theater. She shared with us that the developer's vision was to build a community that had everything its residents could possibly want or need at a short walk's length.

"You won't even have to leave the neighborhood unless you just *want* to." She promised us.

As a parent now myself, I can see the appeal in having everything right there at arm's length. When you're in the middle of cooking dinner for your three kids and realize you're out of milk which just happens to be a key ingredient in the recipe you've already invested all of your meal prep time in and you're at the point of no return, a grocery store right next door to your house would be a savior.

My parents were sold on that first visit. They loved everything about what they were seeing and hearing from that woman. Soon we'd become the very first family to move into the very first house built in our little section of Lake Carolina. It was called Harborside.

From very early on in its design phase, the dream for Harborside was to be a small town community with sidewalks, trees that would one day tunnel its few streets, and the houses would be built so close together you could practically touch your neighbors hand if you happened to both be leaning out of the windows of your neighboring houses towards each other. The houses were so close together and the lots were so small you either loved it or hated it. There was no in between. It felt very stepford wives to me but it must have grown on me. I'd love to move back to that neighborhood today with my own family.

Within a few months of our move into Harborside, it quickly filled in with a colorful array of Charleston-style houses, picket fences, and children riding bikes up and down the sidewalk-lined streets on nice summer evenings. Our yard was teeny tiny with grass that could be cut with two passes of a lawn mower. I'll never forget the one family that moved into a house down the street from us with a riding lawn mower. They either didn't get the memo or they didn't care. Before long, that guy was the talk of the town. Everyone joked that it took him longer to get the riding mower out of his garage and onto the grass than it did to cut the grass itself. It was a ridiculous but entertaining sight to see. The man didn't care. Good for him.

Our house was beautiful. It looked like it was pulled right off of Charleston's Rainbow Row with its pale green exterior and wrap-around porches on the first two of its three stories. The ceilings of both porches were painted sky blue which I thought was an interesting choice by my parents. Who cares about the color of an outdoor porch ceiling? It seems like an odd thing to worry about the aesthetic of. But then they explained to me that it wasn't for the aesthetic. It was a strategic decision—an attempt to keep bugs from building nests on our porch. Since bugs can't build nests in the sky and the sky blue porch ceilings looked like the sky, they wouldn't find that space suitable to build their home. I wonder if bugs really fall for that trick. It is pretty clever if it actually works.

On nice summer evenings before it got too hot and humid outside, we'd have our neighbor friends over for sleepovers on the second story porch. Our neighbors had twin girls, Kate and Paige, who were my age. They quickly became my two best friends. I remember so clearly being able to hear the sound of the fountain water splashing against the concrete at the neighborhood's entrance. That fountain was just a short walk up the road from where we all laid in our sleeping bags – knowing good and well that we wouldn't be spending the entire night out there. As soon as one of us started to feel the slightest drift of an eyelid, we'd scurry together inside and into a real bed. But it was so peaceful laying out there, no care in the world. This house was what we'd always call "the green house."

Even as a young and naive pre-teen, I recognized that we had a fortunate life. That not everyone had to go up three flights of stairs to another story of their house which was entirely designated as their playroom. I knew that both of my parents worked hard to give us the things we had and that house was no exception. In fact, it embodied the privileged life we were living. I have no doubt that back then, I was spoiled by the nice things we'd become accustomed to. I also have no doubt that I was very aware that our life wasn't just handed to us. Was it handed to me and Madeline? Yes, probably. But I knew it wasn't handed to my mom and dad. I knew they both worked extremely hard to give us that life.

For many years, my mom was a very career-oriented woman. By no means did she fit the mold of a lot of the other moms around her or around any of us. She and my dad were both successful young professionals. They each provided close to equal contributions to our household income, especially around this time, in 2002. Their hard work gave us the luxury of living what I would consider to have been an upper middle class lifestyle. We always had the trendiest clothes, rode around in nice cars, and we were given almost anything we could ever want or need any time we asked. I remember I got a laptop for Christmas when we lived in the green house. What does a seventh grader even do with a laptop? Especially back then, before social media really exploded a few years later. I guess AOL Instant Messenger is what I used it for. That's about all I remember using it for at least.

I do think there eventually came a time when my parents realized it probably wasn't a good thing to give us anything and everything we asked for—sometimes before we even asked for them. I think they stopped doing it when they recognized it was starting to have a negative impact on our character. They didn't want us to be so spoiled we couldn't accept no for an answer and no longer appreciated things the way we did before. They didn't want us to feel like we had to leave with something new from every store we walked into. That was the direction it was starting to go. Let me tell you, I had a tough time with their tough love at first. There were lots of tears. I think this is a good use of "first world problems". But parents always know what they're doing.

This was life as I knew it though. In 2002, our little family of four was thriving. Outside of my hard work in school to keep myself on the A, sometimes A/B, honor roll, I played clarinet for the school's band and spent most evenings doing homework in the dance studio between dance classes at *Columbia City Ballet*. I lived the very normal, probably stereotypical, well-rounded life of a middle school girl. Almost every day looked about the same for me, with a few exceptions.

One of my first memorable encounters with my mom's struggle with addiction took place in the green house. I remember exactly where I was, that the sun had already set for the day, and that my hair was wet and freshly brushed from a bath.

They define a core memory as a significant memory that influences your identity behavior, how you see the world. Core memories are usually emotionally intense pivotal moments in your life. This memory with my mom was every bit of a core memory.

2

ambien, my first core memory

Both of my parents traveled for work occasionally in the early 2000s but my dad was gone a lot less frequently than my mom. My mom was a very career-oriented woman, especially throughout her late 20s, 30s, and into her early 40s. I admire this about her now that I'm also a career-oriented woman in my mid-30s. In 2002, when this first core memory of mine occurred, she was 36 years old. This made her just a year older than I am now as I write this book.

On this particular night, the night I'm referring to as my first memorable encounter with my mom being anything but the picture perfect and sober mom I had always known, my dad was out of town on business for a few days. Both my younger sister, Madeline, and I were home with our mom.

Madeline and I have never had a close relationship. For a long time, I blamed it on the fact that we're sisters so close in age, but I've met so many women with sisters just a year or two apart who are best friends. So honestly, I don't really know why it's been so hard between us. We've always just felt like opposites—different in almost every way. Different personalities, different interests, different dreams. Growing up, it felt like we were always fighting. And strangely, that tension still lingers. We used to get into legitimate cat fights. Clawing, scratching, screaming at each other. My dad eventually got us each a pair of boxing gloves. Anytime we'd start fighting, he'd tell us to take it outside and to not come back in until we'd resolved whatever we were fighting about. We eventually stopped the physical altercation but the verbal arguments never stopped. I still have dreams where she's sneaking into my closet while I'm not home, taking my clothes. That was always our biggest battle no matter how much older we got—clothes.

It didn't matter how much we fought, it was still a good thing we had each other. We endured a lot together–including this particular night.

Like I said, my mom was a working mom and Madeline and I were both in school all day so the bulk of our time spent together during the work and school week was in the evenings after school, work, and ballet classes for me.

Now that I'm a mom myself, I see how little time parents, especially working parents, get with their kids each day. It's probably how the truthful and reflective "the days are long but the years are short" saying came to light. It's probably why it's so relatable for so many. The days are long because we work, we go to school, we do activities, we eat, we bathe, and then we go to bed to get the rest we need to do it all over again.

On the average day, the little bit of time carved out for parents to spend time with their kids is filled with homework, dinner planning and prep, wrapping up work calls, and coordinating rides, extracurricular activities, and childcare for the next day. Everyone is already exhausted hours before bedtime so we watch the clock and count down the minutes until we can say goodnight. The days are so long. But then you blink and it's already May and the school year is over. It's time to start looking at childcare plans for the summer and register for kindergarten in the Fall. Where did the time go? It came and went so fast. The years are so fast. I get it now.

On this night, I vividly remember my mom, sister, and I laying in my parents' king-sized bed in their master bedroom of the green house. It was a normal, busy weekday so the time we got to spend together that evening was very limited. American Idol's first season had just aired and that's what we were watching on their bedroom TV. All three of us were fed, bathed, and in our pajamas. We'd just settled down and were relaxing as three before we'd be off to bed an hour or so later.

In the peace of the moment, I remember out of nowhere my mom began saying things that made absolutely no sense. It was so random and unexpected that it took me a few seconds to realize the words were actually coming out of her mouth and they were being directed to us.

"Max *[our dog at the time]* should go on American Idol. He's a great singer, isn't he sweetie?",

"I'm going to finish baking that cake in a few minutes *[at 9:00 p.m. on a school night, there was no cake being baked]*."

There was a lot more than just this. But to give you an idea of the insanity of the sentences coming out of her mouth. These are just two very specific statements that have stuck with me for more than two decades. Everything she said and the entire situation itself was tremendously confusing to me and my sister as we looked at each other and desperately tried to understand what was happening. A 12 year old asking unspoken questions and seeking unspoken answers from her 10 year old little sister and vice versa. Obviously neither of us had answers. It was okay though because we thought she was hilarious. Whatever it was she was doing. Whatever malarkey she was saying. We didn't want it to stop—so we egged her on. We were practically begging her to continue with more unusual thoughts and conversation. We wanted more of this nonsense we had never seen before from our silly mom.

I now wonder what my young, innocent 12 year old brain was thinking in the actual moment while it was happening. I feel certain it would've scared me. At least at first. Moms are supposed to provide protection for their innocent children in our scary world. They are the ones who operate in a state of high alert so that they're ready to jump in and intervene at any sign of threat to their young. That was not the case for my mom on that night. I guess it's a good thing I didn't have the slightest clue what was going on and instead found it entertaining—hilarious even. I never wanted her to stop doing whatever "this" was. They do say ignorance is bliss.

We carried on with her like this for what felt like a long time but was probably only half an hour or so. Our fun was eventually interrupted by a call from my dad to check in. He always called to tell us goodnight and to have pretty dreams. Landlines ("home phones") were still very common in 2002. We had several wireless phones throughout our house and one of them sat on my mom's nightstand right by their bed. It was silver and pretty sleek for its time which is so funny to say now that I'm 20 years in the future where home phones are basically antiques or entirely extinct.

When the phone rang that night, I jumped up quickly to grab it from beside their bed because I knew it would be my dad. I couldn't wait to tell him how funny mommy was being. I remember so clearly telling him about all the crazy things she was saying, my voice filled with laughter and excitement. My dad always did his best to shelter and protect us from worry, from hurt, from danger. Sometimes that meant hiding his own feelings so that he didn't impact ours. I don't recall exactly what he said in response to all this but I'm sure he had no implication of worry in his tone. He would never want us to worry.

Knowing now that it was actually her Ambien talking, I know it wasn't funny to him and I know he was worried. Hearing her like that probably filled him with panic and disappointment. He knew his 10 and 12 year old daughters were at home under solely her care. I can assume he felt helpless being so many miles and likely several flights away from us back at home. I can also assume this wasn't the first time he witnessed behavior like this from her. This certainly wasn't the first night she took Ambien. I'd learn that much later on in life. She probably just managed to hide the side effects from me and my sister until this night. It was a night I'd never forget.

When I first started writing this book and getting all of my big, pivotal moment memories down on paper, I realized something. This problem, her drug addiction, went on a lot longer than I'd always thought. When I was living it, it was easy to lose perspective on elapsed time. As soon as I stepped back to make sense of it all by putting events and dates and years together, it became much more evident how long the timeline actually was.

I don't know if I just became more aware of what was going

on with age but what I'd always thought to be the beginning of her issues was actually when it had gotten bad enough to start creating these core memories for me. I've now discovered that it's more likely this started long before this first memory of mine and this just happened to be when she got not so good at hiding it. It definitely seemed progressive—even if it started before *I* thought it started. I do know that as soon as she got worse at hiding it, she consistently got worse and worse from then on out. When it showed its face to us, its evolution was measurable. But either way, it took time—years—to evolve to what it became. In hindsight, there were so many obvious opportunities for us to jump in and try to stop her before she was beyond repair. The more I dissect my past and the slowly developing tragedy we went through, the more I find myself thinking "what if."

My dad has helped me piece memories together as I've written this book because an accurate timeline feels really important for this story. It's important to see the longevity and severity of the situation to bring perspective to how lucky she was to have even made it through what she did.

While there was a vivid first memory for me of my mom's struggle with addiction, like I alluded to earlier, my dad thinks it's possible it started even earlier than that. He says that looking back, certain situations prior to 2002 make him question his original perception of the timeline of events and how they unfolded. He wonders if she was already starting to experiment with different prescription medications that she probably didn't actually need well before the early 2000s. For reference, my mom had a hysterectomy back in 1999 for severe endometriosis. We think it's possible this surgery first exposed her to the addictive qualities of controlled substances—opioids specifically.

Regardless, by 2002, Ambien was without question a staple in her nightly routine. With an occasional exception here and there, she seemed to have her use of the prescribed sleeping medicine mostly under control. Especially when she followed the doctor's orders. As long as she took it as prescribed and when it was supposed to be taken, she continued to be a high-functioning mom and thriving working professional. It's difficult to pinpoint exactly when it all began. 2002 seems to be a safe and likely place to start.

3

daddy

Any time I hear the phrase "Mr. Mom", I think of my dad and the role he played in our lives growing up. Aside from those occasional work trips he took here and there, he was always close by. Like my mom, my dad also had a very accomplished career. His success was built on hard work and a solid reputation. When our family left Tennessee, which I'll get more into later, his employer extended an offer that allowed him to keep his job at their Nashville-based company and continue his work from our new home in South Carolina. In 1999, the ability to work from home for a company who expects its employees to show up in the office every day in a suit and tie was an opportunity given to my dad years before its time. Something almost unheard of at that point in time.

Now that I've also found myself in Corporate America, I know that kind of freedom and flexibility doesn't just get handed out to anyone. Not even in today's world—where we've lived through a pandemic that gave us no choice but to become more comfortable with and accepting of remote work. I have no doubt it was his strong work ethic and integrity that earned it. He has always been an incredibly hard worker, a perfectionist to his core. I see some of those same defining traits of his in myself. While it's a blessing in many ways to have those innate hard working qualities of a perfectionist, we've both learned on our own time that perfectionism can also be toxic. Always striving to be something, to do something that is just not humanly possible is exhausting.

My dad is an environmental contracts attorney. It's what he did for his job that followed him to South Carolina all those years ago and it's what he still does today. He'll tell anyone that will listen that it's even more boring than it sounds. I don't think it could be much more boring than it sounds. I also don't think it's ever what he would've imagined himself doing for the rest of his life. I have a feeling most of us probably feel this way. I certainly do.

What I saw of my dad's job while I was growing up was that he spent most of his days reading. He was *always* reading. Reading through hundreds of pages of boring legal contracts that he'd print out and physically page through as he scribbled down notes with his black ink BiC pen. He was also always on conference calls. Whatever space in our house we had designated as his office was guaranteed to have giant stacks of paper, sticky notes scattered everywhere, and cups of black ink pens strategically placed in convenient locations where he frequently sat and read.

My dad always had a distinct *work voice* which was much more stern and deep than his *non-work* voice. I can still hear his voicemail greeting in my head when he didn't pick up his work phone.

"Hi, this is Mark Ingram. I can't come to the phone right now..."

We knew we should leave him alone and let him work when we heard his work voice echoing down the halls from his office. A work voice and a dad voice. He was really good at separating but also prioritizing the two, being a dedicated worker and being a dedicated dad, and somehow always succeeded in both.

Daddy's office was always unintentionally but conveniently placed in a room in our house that made it too easy to get to for me and Madeline. I remember walking up to him while he was working at his desk more times than I can count. I always tiptoed because he was almost guaranteed to be on a conference call and quiet steps felt like the least I could do to minimize disruption as much as possible. I knew he wouldn't be happy with me if I tried whispering to him while he was in active conversation so I always resorted to pen and paper instead. I'd ask very non-urgent, insignificant questions that somehow seemed justifiable for interrupting his work day. In fact, I don't ever remember going into his office for an important reason. It was always typical and annoying teenage girl stuff.

"Can I have $20?"

"Can Emily come over and hang out after I finish my homework?"

"What's for dinner? If we don't already have plans, can we pick burgers?"

My questions were always written on a sticky note that I would grab from a pad on his desk. I think about this often on the days I now work out of my own home. I think about how frustrated and annoyed I'd be if I were him. How little patience

I have with my own children when I'm trying to focus on my work and they're climbing up my legs and into my lap, fighting over toys, creating a jungle gym out of our couch cushions. I'm sure my dad felt the same way. But he always gave us what we needed no matter what was going on in his own little world of work or how frustrated he was to be bothered by us. To respond to my questions, he always scribbled his answer on the next line of the sticky note I had placed in front of him and quietly hushed me away with either an eye roll or a smile. It usually depended on his mood and what I was in there for. The point was that he was always there when we needed him, whether he wanted to be or not, he was always the one that was there.

In hindsight, the reality was that my dad didn't really have much of a choice as the parent we'd go running to first. He was always around when my mom wasn't.

For many years, it was work that kept her away. Travel time, conference calls, meetings. She was a business woman in full force. She worked a lot of really long days. She'd be gone long before us in the mornings. Breakfast was often just me, Madeline, and my dad at the kitchen table. Most evenings we'd be long done with dinner and homework when she walked back through the door for the first time since that morning. Still in her pristinely ironed skirt suit with her recently refreshed bright red lipstick, blackberry and leather briefcase in hand. I can still hear the sound of her heels tapping against the hardwoods as she navigated the maze of our house to be able to find us and ask us about our days. Our dogs unable to keep up with her or contain their excitement as they attempted to interlace with her feet, doing everything within the power of their little bodies to get her attention while snagging a run in her pantyhose with their claws.

My mom was undeniably a beautiful woman—the kind of beauty that turned heads and drew compliments from complete strangers. Her eyes were a striking, almost unreal shade of deep blue, like still water under a bright sky, and her strong, defined jawline gave her a natural elegance that no amount of makeup or practiced technique could ever truly replicate. She had a real love for all things girly—makeup, fashion, hair—and she treated it like an art form. She had perfected the delicate technique of layering bold, jet-black mascara on her already long, thick lashes, and she always seemed to pick the perfect shade of red lipstick to highlight her full, symmetrical lips. Her sense of style was effortless yet bold, always a few steps ahead of whatever trend was popular at the time.

Photos from the early 90s show her in high-waisted, barrel-leg jeans, crisp white Keds, and slouchy crew socks—an outfit that feels just as current today as it did back then. In almost every photo, she looks like she stepped right out of a fashion magazine. That's the kind of beauty she carried, the kind that seemed timeless, magnetic, and entirely her own.

There was no question that at the peak of her success, in all aspects of her life, my mom was a woman of power and ambition. People respected her, they admired her, some even envied her. She had unmatched grit and determination. She was a presence—unmistakable and commanding—and carried herself with a quiet confidence and poise that turned heads the moment she entered a room. I knew I wanted to be just like her one day.

But my dad was the quiet hero in the background—the steady, unwavering presence who rarely asked for recognition but whose support made everything possible. While my mom was the one in the spotlight, pursuing her ambitions and building her success, it was my dad who held everything else together. He made countless sacrifices, often setting his own needs aside to make sure she had the space, stability, and encouragement to thrive. The truth is, much of what she achieved wouldn't have been possible without him—and he deserves far more credit than he ever received. It's hard work in itself just raising kids. Balancing that while trying to grow in your own career—especially when you and your partner are both chasing the same kind of success—can feel nearly impossible.

With kids, the reality is that it's just not possible for both parents to prioritize their work, above everything else, all the time. No matter what, being a parent and being there for your child is your biggest job. Your most important responsibility. But that doesn't always mean both parents have to stop what they're doing, drop their work, to be a parent. In fact, in most cases, it makes the most sense for one parent to agree to work and one parent to agree to parent. My dad was usually that parent—the one that volunteered to parent. He was the parent who most often made sacrifices in his career so that my mom could succeed. He would always do anything and everything within his power to help her succeed and to make sure we were taken care of.

I do appreciate everything he did for us. I didn't see it or understand it while it was happening. I hate that I didn't. I wish I could go back to every single one of those moments and tell him how much I appreciated him. Unfortunately, we have yet to figure out time travel. Making sure he feels appreciated now is all I can do. I know that even today, if he had to go back and do it again, he'd do it all again and again without a second thought. My sister and I were his priority. We always were and we still are. Even as grown women with children of our own.

My dad has always put everyone else's wants and needs before his own. It seems to just be in his nature. A genuinely good person. Whether the sacrifice was big or small, he never hesitates. It's just part of how he shows love. He's always done whatever it takes to keep our family afloat. He's a selfless man like that. A true Mr. Mom.

4

the crack that crumbled the foundation

2003

In the early part of 2003, while we were still living in the little green house, my mom endured the heartbreak of losing a job for the first time — a moment that quietly marked the beginning of a much heavier chapter in her life. It was entirely unforeseen so when it happened, it was understandably and predictably detrimental.

The company she worked for that ultimately led our relocation back to South Carolina from Tennessee in 1999 was acquired by another organization. This resulted in mass layoffs which isn't uncommon when a situation like this unfolds. Unfortunately, like many of her close counterparts, my mom's job wasn't spared when this happened. She took the news extremely hard, as would anyone when confronted with their first perceived failure after only knowing success most of their life. It wasn't her fault or anything she did wrong, even she knew that. But the quickest person to blame here was herself and that's exactly what she did.

I think about this and wish I could go back to my younger self and explain how much my mom needed me when this happened. Not that I was old enough or mature enough to be able to say something to make things better. But I still could've been there for her. She needed any bit of reassurance and support she could get when this happened. She needed to be reminded by anyone she'd be willing to listen to that everything was going to be okay. That so many people looked up to her and admired all the things that made her who she was. That bad things happen to good people sometimes but there are sure to be better days ahead. But I was young and dumb, selfish, and oblivious. So I didn't say a word to her about it. I didn't have the slightest clue what it meant when she lost that job or how much it actually affected her.

I wish I could go back and give her a hug, the way she'd hug me today if she were still here and the same thing were to happen to me. I wish I could wrap my arms around her and remind her that everything is going to be okay. Maybe that one little hug, that one little sentence of affirmation and support, could've changed everything.

My dad said losing this job destroyed her. It destroyed her so much that it's his strong belief that this was *the* gateway that led her to find comfort in prescription medications. *This* is when she began to use them for more than they were ever intended. *This* is when she began to abuse them. For my mom, her identity and her worth were both largely defined by the success she achieved in her career. The problem with that and dedicating so much of herself to her work was that losing her job caused her to lose sight of who she was and what her real purpose was.

The impact of this loss was significant for our family too. For the first time in our entire 13 years of being a family, we were required to rely on a single income. But it was more than just having to rely on a single income – it was having to live on a single income in a house mortgaged for two. An entire life built for two. It wasn't a financial situation my parents could maintain without making sacrifices of things they felt were higher priority necessities in our lives – dance classes for me, Sylvan learning sessions for Madeline, the two cars my parents drove, among others. All those things they identified as higher priority necessities were carefully considered, critiqued, and ultimately chosen as essentials that they just didn't want us to have to live without. But something, somewhere had to give.

So the decision was made. Just like that, we were leaving our beautiful green house in Harborside and the best neighborhood community we'd ever been a part of. All of it was over. We were walking away. The second story porch sleepovers. The neighborhood cookouts and fireworks on the 4th of July. The ease of access in sharing clothes with my two best friends' five houses down the road. The beautiful water fountain that welcomed us and waved us goodbye every time we came and went. It was all over. There were so many good memories I never got the chance to make. Memories none of us got a chance to make in that short year we were given with our lovely green house.

I was utterly heartbroken to leave but in hindsight, I'm willing to bet my parents, especially my mom, were even more heartbroken. They never cried in front of us or anything but you could see it in their eyes. You could catch it in the subtle undertone of their voices—a quiet disappointment tucked beneath the certainty with which they shared their plans. They did their best to give us just enough information and reasoning to make sense of our move out of the green house without prompting worry or concern. That childhood bubble they continued to protect with every last breath. And while we were too young to be brought into the reality of what was struggling finances, we were old enough to be resentful towards them. Resentful that we were being taken so quickly from a house we had equally as quickly grown to love. Resentful that we had no say in going or staying. I wouldn't know the truth behind this move and why it had to happen for many, many years. There's both grace and tragedy in the way children are often shielded from harsh realities. In their quiet sacrifice, parents absorb the weight of pain and blame—sacrificing themselves, choosing to bear it alone if it means preserving their children's sense of safety. It's a profound act of love, though rarely recognized in the moment or many years thereafter.

These were my selfish, stupid thoughts at 13:

Everything was perfect at the green house. We were all so happy. We love this neighborhood. So what if mommy lost her job? She can find another one. Isn't that what adults do? They find another job when the first one doesn't work out. There are tons of jobs out there. They're all over the newspaper, on TV. Heck, they're even on billboards. There's no shortage of them. It really can't be that hard.

They say they want to move to a house with a larger backyard. They've never cared about the size of our backyard here. We have the same two dogs now that we had when they chose this house with the tiny backyard. Plus, they love it here. All they've ever said is how much they love it here. They said it themselves this has been their favorite house we've ever lived in. It makes no sense. They drive me crazy. It's always about them and whatever they want.

I'm so angry with them. I hate this. I'll never forgive them.

Meanwhile, this was one of the hardest decisions they've ever had to make. Especially as parents themselves. My mom was on job sites the very night she got laid off, with a tissue box placed right beside her lap so that she could catch any tears that managed to escape while she scrolled *Indeed.com*. She was doing everything she could to find another job. Even if it wasn't something she wanted to do long term. Something temporary. Anything.

She and my dad both lost weeks of sleep. Tossing and turning for hours all throughout the night so that they could wake up with their alarm and put on a smile for me and Madeline. They went back and forth over their budget trying to figure out how to make this work—how to save a dollar here and a dollar there to keep us in the green house. They started clipping coupons for the first time in their lives and bringing those along with us on our grocery shopping trips. I'd ask what they were because I had not personally seen a paper coupon in my life. They started buying store brand foods in place of the name brands that always filled our pantry. We started going to Walmart instead of Target. Kroger instead of Publix. They did all of this while they desperately held onto hope that a recruiter would call with a job offer that saved us and let us keep the life we always knew. But eventually they realized they had no choice. They couldn't make this work for any longer. Finding a job clearly wasn't as easy as losing one. We had to move to a more affordable house.

My mom was devastated at the thought of upsetting us. She knew how happy we were in the green house. She felt so guilty. This was all her fault. But they had to come up with something to tell us to let us down as easily as possible. They didn't want to hurt us or have us worry over the things they were worrying over. A bigger backyard would be a perfectly logical reason to want to move. We had two dogs, it made sense. The almost nonexistent yard at the green house definitely wasn't reasonable with two dogs even if it seemed that way when we bought the house. Now we had experienced that small backyard for long enough for validation that it just wouldn't work for our dog situation.

So that's what they told us. That's the only story I ever heard until I started writing this book.

5

a pepto bismol pink bedroom

Our next house was underwhelming. I don't remember much about it other than that it was a two-story, brick house. It sat alone on a very empty cul-de-sac. I don't know why the house sat by itself, there was plenty of room for more houses around it. In Harborside, there would've been eight houses lining that same cul-de-sac. But not in this neighborhood. It was just our house with our nonexistent neighbor friends. I remember the day we moved in, the grass in our yard was patchy and dead. It was fitting for the overwhelming feelings of dread and disappointment I carried along with me that whole day.

I don't remember making friends in the neighborhood or even interacting with any of our neighbors. It was a totally different atmosphere from Harborside. There was nothing special about it in comparison to where we came from. Before I even gave this house a chance to impress me, my mind was made up. I didn't like being there and I never would.

This was the house with the pepto bismol pink bedroom I mentioned earlier on. *My* pepto bismol pink bedroom. Before we bought the house, the room was the boring pale yellow you'd see in a lot of houses in the early 2000s. Probably what most are calling and loving "butter yellow" nowadays. But not for long. Not if I had anything to do with it.

If it was dark outside and my bedroom light was on, you could literally see the pink radiating through every little fiber of the curtain panels as you were driving up to our house. Maybe even before that – when you were driving down our road. It was obscene. It looked like one of those star projectors you'd buy on Amazon. But all the stars were pink. I can only imagine how hard my mom had to bite her tongue when she saw the color I had picked out as I proudly handed her that paint swatch in the paint aisle of Home Depot. I know why she did it though. She wanted me to be happy. If painting my room an obnoxious paint color was what it took to make me happy, she was willing to sacrifice the aesthetic of one upstairs room to give me that.

It seems silly, a room color. I sound a bit dramatic to consider this a selfless act of my mom's. Letting me pick out my own bedroom color. Like it's such a big deal that she let me do it. I talk about it like she was a saint for doing it. Paint can easily be covered up. It's far from permanent. It sounds insignificant, comical even. But it really was a big deal for her. I know how hard it was for her and I genuinely respect her for it.

Now that I really understand the sacrifice in little things like keeping her word and actually painting my bedroom the awful color I picked out because she told me I could pick it out and she meant it, I wish I could go back and tell her thank you.

This is the kind of mom she always was—sober or not—and it's also why we grew so close the older I got. It was impossible not to love her. It was impossible not to recognize the genuinely good human she was. Impossible not to feel loved by her. She always did little thoughtful things like this, things that I really grew to appreciate, the more I understood how *big* these little things actually were for her. Sadly, it took many years for me to see these little things through this lens. As big things. But she was doing it all along. She didn't need to be seen or understood. She didn't need to feel appreciated by us to want to continue doing all the things she'd always done for us. What made her happiest was loving us. Giving to us. Seeing us happy. I wouldn't be able to count the number of times I was told growing up, in reference to my mom, "you girls are her world." I believe it. I know we were. She was mine too.

Aside from my pepto bismol room, our time in that house was mostly uneventful, from what I can recall at least. The only big memory I have living in this brick house was actually outside of the brick house. It was the day my dad took me in his car and tried to teach me how to drive. I say car but I don't mean a literal car. We were actually in a white Trailblazer SUV. I have a funny story about that Trailblazer actually.

One evening we pulled into our driveway after returning home from a Saturday movie outing, the four of us. As my dad parked the car and we all unbuckled, my sister and I were arguing over something. Somehow, some way, in the process of our argument, a piece of gum fell out of my mouth and my sister accidentally smeared it into the backseat carpet. My dad was livid. If it was entirely accidental, I don't think he would've been but he knew we were arguing and being reckless. Because of that, he was in fumes.

He raised his voice and told us, "I don't care how long the two of you are out here or what you have to do to clean it up, neither of you are coming inside until that gum is OUT of the carpet."

Keep in mind, we didn't have internet service on cell phones at this point. At least not on the pink Nokia cell phone I had. We tried everything we thought may do the trick but nothing was working. Finally, I walked into the garage and walked back out to the car to meet my sister with a pair of scissors. Nothing else was working but I guaranteed her scissors would do the trick. Just as you may have guessed, we cut the entire gum-covered portion of the carpet out of the backseat flooring within a couple minutes. If only we had thought of that solution sooner. We wouldn't have been out there for over an hour. Once the gum was completely gone, we proudly went inside and grabbed our dad to show off our hard work. He was angry with us for weeks after that. To this day, I remind him that he *did* say, "I don't care what you have to do to get it out." I've always been a very literal person. I was just following his direction and being resourceful.

Anyway, back to the Trailblazer. I feel like I need to give some context here on the size of the vehicle before I dive into the driving story. I don't want to get ahead of myself and give credit where credit's deserved. Because I will never forget how terribly I drove the first time I got behind the steering wheel of that Trailblazer.

I never thought in a million years it would be as difficult as it felt that day to keep a car on the road. I could feel my dad's stress and frustration radiating throughout the car as he sat there quietly but tensely beside me. I could see his thumb tapping against his lap which usually meant it was anxious. I won't lie, I was equally surprised with how bad of a driver I was. It had always looked so easy.

I remember getting so frustrated I pulled the car over and told my dad I was done and I wanted to go home. I was angry with myself but I was also embarrassed and disappointed. I never handled struggle well. I wanted to be good at everything the first time. I probably cried all two minutes of that drive home too. I really didn't like to be bad at things. Plus, I was always a bit dramatic. My dad can tell you that himself.

A few weeks later, we tried again and it was completely different the second time around. It was like something just clicked and I drove as if I'd been driving my whole life. I say that as I laugh to myself because I'm sure my dad was very much still scared for his life and traumatized from our last car ride. But he still got in the car with me again, without hesitation, because he wasn't going to give up on me and most definitely wasn't going to let me give up on myself.

This really is all I can remember from our time in this brick house. I guess it didn't make a big impression on me. This house never really found its way into conversations like some of our other houses did for many years after we had moved on. Except that story of my first time driving. That story has definitely come up in quite a few conversations over family dinner. It never had a real nickname either. It was just the house with the pepto bismol pink room. We never stopped missing Harborside.

Some time in early 2004, my parents spontaneously decided to try something new and completely different from anything they'd done in the past. I say spontaneous but I'm sure there was a lot of planning and hard decisions made behind the scenes to ultimately decide this was something worth trying. Neither of my parents took any decision lightly or made any change halfheartedly. If we were doing something, it was carefully and seriously thought through. Like most other big changes in our lives at this time, by the time the news made its way to us, it was a done deal. They were starting their own real estate business.

While my mom completed online courses and passed a series of tests to become a licensed real estate agent, my dad did the same to become a licensed real estate broker. His process to become a broker was more straightforward because he was already a licensed attorney. So with their powers and newly acquired licenses combined, they created *the home shoppe, llc*. I remember my dad was so proud of the logo he designed himself (just like the cover of this book) for their business cards and office signage. It was a simple logo with a rope swing hanging from a branch of an established oak tree. Their color palette was simple too. Navy and white. The business cards were matte white with the logo and "the home shoppe, llc" printed in navy across the bottom. My dad was proud of those business cards. He still has a few of them that he's held onto ever since.

I think both of my parents really enjoyed their venture into real estate. There was a lot of excitement in it being so different and new, especially at first. Their game plan was for my mom to do this for a living, as her primary profession, and my dad would continue with his career in contracts law and do real estate brokerage on the side. Ideally he'd oversee and step in when it was necessary for their operations. It was a plan that worked well for them. It gave my dad a small taste of something different that didn't bore him to death like reading legal contracts. Though he probably still did a bit of that as a broker. It gave my mom room for creativity and flexibility she would never find in Corporate America. Even better than that, all of her "work time" now revolved around houses. What she loved most. My parents had always had a deep love for all things home-related—design, construction, renovation, you name it. They loved it all. My mom also had the personality to do well in real estate. She was always the social butterfly and extrovert of the family. People were drawn to her which helps when you're in sales.

I remember so many Sunday afternoons, even long before their real estate endeavor, we'd drive around for hours just looking at houses. I never understood what that even meant — to go "looking at houses" — but that's always what they called this Sunday afternoon family activity of ours. It definitely made them happy. Their moods were always top notch on these Sunday drives. Looking at houses seemed almost therapeutic for them.

When things started to get really bad for my mom, my dad would randomly go out for drives and look at houses.

He'd find his way to the front door and quietly say to us, "I'm going for a drive. I'll be back later."

Except these times were by himself. Doing one of the many things they used to love doing together. He really did seem to find healing in houses. Madeline and I would usually both cry to each other in fear of him never coming back as we sat in the living room and stared at the front door. Celebrating in silence when we saw his headlights pulling up to our house. But we weren't to this point just yet. Looking at houses was still a hobby we did as a full family.

On many of these Sunday afternoon excursions we'd never even step foot out of the car. It was the strangest thing. We'd slow down and possibly even come to a stop if they wanted a longer "look" at a house that piqued their interest in some sort but then we'd be on our way again. But there were two guaranteed exceptions to this that would absolutely get us out of the car. Those two exceptions were passing an open house sign planted in the yard of a property that appealed to them or an active build that was still in the framing stage of construction and therefore easily accessible for bystanders and imaginative minds. If we crossed paths with either of the two, we were almost 100% guaranteed to go inside.

My sister and I would complain the entire time. It was the epitome of boredom for us. She and I never had a whole lot in common. In fact, we fought more than we got along. But we were always equally annoyed by the things we'd get dragged along to do. My parents didn't care though, this stuff made them happy. And even if we were sitting in the backseat complaining the entire time, asking incessantly when we could go back home, nothing made my mom happier than having all four of us together.

6

the red house

2004-2008

Nine short months later, my parents sat us down in the living room of the pepto bismol pink bedroom house and told us they missed Harborside too much and they were moving us back. I guess the bigger yard wasn't all it was cracked up to be after all. The reality was, unknowingly to us, their new real estate business was doing really well. As soon as they could afford it and make it make financial sense again, they were ready to move us back to where they wished we could've stayed put all along.

We weren't in that brick house on the other side of town for long before we found ourselves back in Harborside. Yes, that's right, we were right back in Harborside. Literally nine months after we left. Might I remind you, this community was really small. There were just a small handful of streets running through it to accommodate the tightly knit placement of its colorful array of houses. The funny thing was, we weren't just back in Harborside. That makes it sound less peculiar than it actually was. We were back in Harborside and on the same street, just three houses down, from the green house. The green house street number was 201 and our new street number was 207. Literally three houses down. I can only imagine how confused our neighbors were. I was right there with them. It didn't have to make sense to me though, I was just happy to be back.

It would've been early 2004 when we were welcomed by our old/new neighbors back to Harborside. For the second time. The second house was a two-story, arts and crafts style home with a barn red exterior. This house also sat on an extremely small lot, just like the green house. Each house on our street had a small strip of grass out front. This strip of grass served as the "front yard" and separated each house from the sidewalk which ran through Lake Carolina Boulevard, our street.

The majority of our grass here sat back behind the house situated between the house itself and a detached garage with a finished room above it. A "FROG" (finished room above garage). My dad managed to somehow turn that tiny little "backyard" into what felt like a secret garden straight from a magazine. Beautiful flowers lined almost every square foot of the outdoor space and the pebble pathway that connected the garage and house structures. There was a reading bench which sat in a shaded spot overlooking the garden and a hummingbird feeder to welcome the winged visitors. All of that and there was still just enough free space for me to one day practice my back handsprings in that little backyard.

A year or so into living in this red house, my dad repainted the entire exterior by himself. I remember it being a lot of work—like most of the projects he'd decide to endeavor those days.

Anyone else would've called him crazy for taking on such a big task by himself. He'd dismiss the commentary and proceed stubbornly with the "one man" job not actually intended for one man. He'd get just far enough into the project where there was no turning back when he'd realize it was definitely too much for one person. This is when his mood would shift. The initial excitement had long worn off and things were taking way longer than he thought they would. From that point on, until the project was finished, any minute he spent thinking about it or working on it was done grumpily. But he was stubborn – he'd never leave a task unfinished. Especially not painting the exterior of a house. He had no choice but to finish this one. So he'd carry on in his grumpiness and we'd leave him alone because we knew it was best to leave him alone when he got in these moods. We just needed to leave him alone and let him finish. As soon as he was done, he'd be peppy again.

The new exterior color was a different shade of green than "the green house" but it was also green. Man, they must've *really* missed that green house. I know they had to go through a lot of approvals with the homeowners association to even be able to change the house color. You even had to get HOA approvals to plant plants in the ground of your own property. A little intense if you ask me. With that in mind, it's somewhat shocking they were open to the idea of changing a house color—especially on a house that sat on the main street of our section. I guess each color that lined the street had to be cohesive and make sense. Or the HOA just wanted control. It was probably that.

Since we already had a green house, we couldn't have another green house. That would be way too confusing to keep up with in conversation or, you know, while reading a book. Since this house was at one point in time a red house, we would always call it "the red house." Confusing I know. Even though we spent more time in the red house as a green house, I still picture it with that barn red exterior. I always will. It will always be the red house to me.

The red house was where my mom's occasional use of more medication than she was prescribed would inevitably turn into a full blown and deadly battle with addiction. The red house will always be *that* for me. I'm not sure when it stopped just being those occasional funny interactions we'd have with her when she took her Ambien too long before bed. But at some point while we were living in the red house, things escalated astronomically. Without even recognizing it, it happened right there before our eyes.

There were sad times here, lots of them, but there were happy times too. The red house is where we lived the entire time I was in high school. So many of my best memories from those years happened while we were living here. This is where I called home when I danced in the Nutcracker and where I got ready for my junior and senior year proms. It's where I parked my first car every night along the street in front of our house and where I'd get caught sneaking out more times than I'll ever admit to my own children. This is the house that my Clemson acceptance letter was addressed to and where I thought I was dying of a broken heart before I actually fell in love for the first time. For so many reasons, so many accomplishments and failures, so many laughs and tears, so many rights and wrongs, the red house was the most sentimental of all of our houses to me. It holds the biggest place in my heart because of the hardships we went through between those walls. I lost my mom on paper in 2015 but the reality was, I lost her a long time before that. I lost her here, in this house. The red house is the house that broke me.

In 2005, I made our high school's varsity cheerleading squad. This was an unexpected turn of events for me because ballet had always been my biggest passion in life. I'm not sure what even enticed me to try out for cheerleading. I have very little recollection of contemplating the decision, try outs, anything like that. I just remember finding out I made the team and being pleasantly shocked. Looking back, it seems so random. I was still dancing when I tried out for cheerleading. I didn't go into it with high expectations of actually making the team. When I did, the reality of the tough decision to follow—dance or cheerleading—hit me with a pit in my stomach. I knew to be able to commit to one, I had to quit the other. There was no way to do both. Both were extremely time consuming. I suppose my social standing took precedence and ultimately influenced me to choose cheerleading over dance. I still find myself wondering, even to this day, if that was the right decision.

Cheerleading was a huge part of my life in high school but it's not really relevant for this story. I only mention it because my mom never fought me in my decision to quit dancing which is crazy to even say. Looking back, it makes me sad that she never tried to talk me out of it. Dance always meant a lot to me but it also meant a lot to her. It probably meant even more to her. She loved watching me dance. Dance was something I had done my entire life - since I was three years old when I got dressed up in a bright yellow duck costume tapping away at my first recital. She'd tell me years later that I screamed the entire hour of my first five dance classes. She'd offer to take me out but the instructor would reassure her it was normal, it took time for some children to adjust. She promised my mom

I'd surprise her one day by walking in and not looking back for once. She was right, I'm glad my mom listened. I grew to love it very soon after that. From three years old until I was fifteen, dance was the biggest love of my life.

I wanted to tell myself my mom was just letting me be responsible for my own decisions but I knew her better than that. She was opinionated. She would've felt like the discipline and structure of dance was what was best for me, especially in those high school years. When kids are exposed to many of their firsts, peer pressured to do things they've never done. I just know she would've done everything within her power to keep me dancing. At least that's what she would've done before addiction. The mom I had when I made the varsity cheerleading squad didn't try to talk me out of quitting dance because addiction had already begun to take over who she was. She was no longer the same person that anxiously waited outside of my preschool dance class to give me a big hug and tell me how proud she was. Thankfully she was that person at one point in time. She was the person that always pushed me to do the things she knew I'd thank her for when I was old enough to understand. She wouldn't let me give up that easily. She always believed in me.

Cheerleading was probably the best thing that could've happened to me in high school regardless of whether or not it was the right or wrong decision at the time. It kept me busy throughout the school year and most of the summer and introduced me to the girls I'd always refer to as my high school best friends. The same girls that would sadly and unknowingly become my biggest support system at just sixteen years old. Cheerleading was the one part of my life I could count on for normalcy. Just like all the other girls on the squad, I went to after-school practices, summer clinics, cheer competitions, and football games. When I was off doing these things, my life no different than theirs. Things felt normal. The difference between them and me was that normalcy followed them back to their homes. I didn't have that luxury. Home, for me, was the one place that didn't feel normal anymore. Home was no longer my safe place.

My parents' real estate business eventually fizzled out as their house closings and resulting commissions slowed down. They eventually realized the income real estate was bringing in for them just wasn't reliable or consistent enough for them to feel comfortable relying on it as a primary source for supporting our living expenses. My mom decided stability made the most sense and because of that, she found herself back in Corporate America in 2006.

I was a sophomore in high school in 2006. 16 years old. I feel like I spent my freshman year figuring out how I wanted to look, to dress, to do my hair and makeup so by my freshman year, I was a less awkward, more confident young woman. I regularly saw a hairstylist at a very expensive hair salon downtown by this point in my life. That's the only way I had the bright blonde hair that I did all throughout high school and most of college. Only a professional could create that from that dishwater blonde they covered in highlights. Side bangs were in style in 2006 so it only made sense for me to have them. Unfortunately tanning beds were also the thing to do in 2006 and my parents despised them. I somehow talked my way into having a membership at Ultra Tan in short bursts throughout the school year which is the only reason my skin had any color other than my natural shade of pale. Tanning beds are now one of my biggest regrets in life.

When my mom made the decision to go back into full time work, the solid reputation she built leading up to 2006 allowed her to lean on her professional network of peers for referrals. Fortunately for her, real estate was still enough to relieve some of the sense of urgency in finding something new. This gave her more time for outreach to her connections across the healthcare industry which inevitably got her foot in the door at an insurance company as an IT project manager.

Apparently my mom never had any of the official project management certifications you see as requirements in most project management positions nowadays. My dad said she never needed them. At least not back then. It might've been a different story in today's times. She was incredibly good at her job. She was organized, well-spoken, effective at managing people, and just easy to work with. People just enjoyed working with her. This was not to be confused with her being a yes woman, she was anything but that. She was a force, remember? You don't get that reputation by saying yes to everyone and everything. She was the perfect balance of tough and approachable. It's interesting to think about what made her such a good project manager. I never had any appreciation for it back then. I didn't have much appreciation for anything that didn't immediately interest me those years. I had no idea what a project manager was until I became a working professional myself. The funny thing is that I'm told all the time by people who never knew my mom how great of a project manager I'd be for all the same reasons my mom was so good at her job. I guess the apple doesn't fall far.

She seemed to be doing well in her new job at first. It was nice to see her back in her natural habitat. Real estate worked for her but she definitely thrived in Corporate America. I think we all had similar feelings on that. She carried herself with a renewed sense of purpose once she was back in those pinstripe pantsuits and high heel shoes. She held her head a little higher and had a new pep in her step. It was easy to see she was back where she belonged.

My mom built friendships with her coworkers quickly at that new company. My dad said it wasn't uncommon for her to make quick friendships, even at work. She was easy to like and it's even easier to like a coworker you respect as a professional as well. Successful professionals attract successful professionals. That's just how it works. This is how she found herself invited to a Christmas party at one of the executives houses a night in early December 2006.

On this particular evening, the night of the Christmas party event, my mom had driven straight from work over to her coworker's house. She worked such long days, it made logical sense for the party to begin right as she was getting off of work. She was there for a while before my dad got a call from her asking if he could come pick her up. It was a little unusual but he assumed they were probably serving alcohol wherever she was. She told him she wasn't able to drive herself home— that she wasn't in a state to get behind the wheel. My dad assumed she had just had a few too many cocktails was a bit surprised she was already wanting to come home. She always enjoyed social gatherings and wasn't known to be the first to leave a party. She was a social drinker but never did anything crazy. She definitely wouldn't have intentionally gotten drunk in front of coworkers. My dad said his first impression was that it was all a bit strange. But he appreciated she was making the smart decision to not get behind the wheel so he got into his car and headed her way.

As soon as he pulled up to get her, she was outside waiting. It was a bit unexpected because it was cold outside and it didn't seem necessary to stand there waiting not knowing exactly when he'd arrive. Plus she was still in a dress and heels from work that day. As soon as his car was close enough for him to see her face, he knew she was severely intoxicated. She had a blank stare, her shoulders were slouched, her stance was off balance. When she got in the car, my dad found it hard to comprehend the state she was in. He said the only way to describe it was as if she had mixed alcohol with some sort of powerful medication. Her speech was slurred, she was falling asleep mid-sentence, her conversation was incoherent. She wasn't just drunk. It was much different than that.

They picked up her car the next morning. It was still parked on the street outside of her co-worker's house. They didn't speak a word of that night after that. A few days later, her work contract was unexpectedly terminated. She could never give my dad an explanation which was every bit of suspicious. We don't know what happened that night at the Christmas party before she called my dad to pick her up but it seems likely it was detrimental to both her reputation and to her career. Everything seemed to go downhill quickly from that point on.

Most of my darkest memories with my mom were during my junior and senior years of high school in that red house. As I was growing old enough to really understand what was going on around me, her battle with addiction was continuing to get worse. The evolution of those two realities—my maturing and her addiction—advancing quickly and in parallel is what eventually opened my eyes to the truth of who my mom had become

Around this time was also when it was relatively common

for me to have my own company over to our house. Friends would come over to spend the night. My boyfriend and I would watch movies in the living room. Just normal teenage things. They were frequently at our house. Our finished room above the detached garage made it an ideal spot for hanging out at our age. The physical separation gave us a sense of freedom and privacy. Everyone liked coming to our house.

The only problem was that meant what was previously happening behind closed doors, only for our little family of four to see, became much harder to hide. By that point, anyone in their right mind that had any sort of situational awareness would know my mom was almost always high. They may not have known *what* she was high on but that little detail was pretty insignificant. The point was that it wasn't normal, *she* wasn't normal. Anyone who interacted with her when she was in that state of mind knew she had something going on. It humiliated me. I was afraid people would judge me for the behaviors of my mom, judge our family. I was ashamed of who she was and my only sense of peace was found in her absence. When she wasn't around to make a fool of herself. To make a fool of me.

All of that to say, I was becoming more used to it. More used to holding my breath and crossing my fingers when she'd come out of her bedroom while a friend was over, praying that she'd just keep to herself and not open her mouth. More used to feeling that huge sense of relief when I knew she was passed out in her bedroom with very little chance of her coming out while my friends were over.

What "it" was, I still wasn't entirely sure. Not yet anyway. I mean, I had a general idea from context clues. She'd go into her purse to grab pills from various prescription bottles and at that point, we knew we had about an hour before the odd behavior would begin. I kind of knew what was going on.

One day, my boyfriend was over and asked me if I knew where my mom kept her pills. I remember it caught me completely off guard. What pills? He explained that she was clearly on something, he wanted to know what it was. I mean yeah, that much was obvious. I guess I'd never thought to investigate it myself. My best guess was that she kept anything like that in her purse so I brought it to him. I guess she wasn't anywhere around when this was happening because I don't remember being the slightest bit worried she'd walk in and get mad. Either that or I just didn't yet understand the private life she was living that she stored in that purse. She absolutely would not have wanted anyone to go digging in there uninvited.

I don't remember exactly what the pill bottles were labeled with but I remember it being medication names easily recognizable by teenagers our age. Probably drugs Lil Wayne introduced us to in his music. This was the day I realized how naive I was to what she was doing. I couldn't believe how clueless I really was. It had never crossed my mind to try to find out what all those medications actually were. He had more common sense than me I guess. Or I had always just lived such a sheltered life in my childhood bubble. My mom's purse was for car keys, money, and lipstick—the last place I'd expect to find hardcore narcotics.

What we found that day kind of just helped paint the rest of the picture of what I already knew was going on. Seeing her high on prescription medications had just become standard operating procedure, more or less. It was expected enough that I woke up every morning and my first thought was wondering if she'd be sober or incoherent that day. Sober would be a pleasant surprise. At seventeen years old, while my friends were stressing over which party to go to that Friday night, what outfit to wear that day to school, I was worrying over my dad's increasingly obvious sadness and the well-being of my mom's life. But it's all I ever knew those years. I had no idea how hard my life was in comparison to most people my age. I didn't have the slightest clue how much strength I had to possess each morning I woke up, in comparison to all the other seventeen year old girls around me, just to be able to get through each day.

After my mom lost her job "unexpectedly" following the mysterious Christmas party incident, every job she had thereafter eventually followed suit. She'd get a job, lose the job, get a job, lose the job. Some would last a little longer than others but the outcome was always the same. While it was happening, I remember it feeling unusual that my mom could be so unlucky. To keep losing all these jobs. For each of these new companies to just happen to need to do mass layoffs shortly after she came onboard. But that's all they ever told us. "Your mom was laid off today. She'll start looking for another job tomorrow." Apparently I was aware of her addiction but never put two and two together that she was taking all of that to work with her as well. I guess I wanted to believe that she was a different woman when she walked out our front door every morning for work. That's what I chose to believe.

I remember asking my dad if a layoff was different from being fired. I didn't know the difference between the two terms but fired sounded a lot more serious. Like she did something wrong. "No sweetie, the company was doing layoffs. Mommy didn't get fired" he'd reassure me. I believed anything he said.

7

first the faucet dripped, then the ceiling caved

a series of unfortunate events

There were numerous incidents that took place in the red house—each one tied, in some way, to my mom's deepening struggle with prescription drug abuse. By that stage, addiction wasn't just a problem for her—it had become a way of life. Because of that, our home became a backdrop for a seemingly endless stream of hardship and emotional chaos.

Although many days blurred together in a haze of repetition and dysfunction, I believe it's important to highlight certain moments—specific events that stood out not only for their intensity, but for what they revealed about the depth of her addiction and the toll it took on all of us.

There were three particularly distressing events that occurred within a relatively short span of time. I want to share each of them with you, because I believe doing so will paint a clearer picture of just how far things had unraveled, and how severe her condition truly was.

event one

One late summer evening in May 2007, shortly after my mom walked into the red house from work, someone knocked on our front door.

My parents both parked their cars in our detached garage behind the house. By the time you parked, locked up the garage, walked through the backyard and eventually made your way through the back door into the kitchen, it had been several minutes since your initial arrival back home. Sometimes my mom would stay in her car and wrap up a phone call before she actually make her way inside and sometimes she'd come right in.

It was strange that we'd have an unexpected visitor at our door on a weeknight. My mom didn't mention seeing anyone pull up to our house when she was passing by right before that herself to make her way to our garage.

My dad made his way to the door where he was greeted by two officers from the local sheriff's department. They looked equally surprised as he was. Even though it was our house, not theirs. My dad didn't have any time to try to comprehend what was going on and why there would be two police officers standing on our porch before they started talking. My sister and I were both home safely and my mom had just gotten home herself so he knew we were all where we needed to be. At least he knew they weren't there to deliver any devastating news, the way you see them do on TV shows.

One of the officers quickly began to speak. There was no sense in wasting time, they had other places to be. He proceeded to tell my dad that a civilian had called in and reported a vehicle driving very recklessly, hitting multiple medians and swerving in and out of lanes for many miles in high traffic areas. The other officer added that the civilian who called 911 had followed the reckless driver home so that he could get their address and report it to the police. That address is what brought them to our front door. The police asked who in our house would've been driving the silver Toyota Camry that was seen pulling into the garage a few minutes prior. It was my mom of course, there was no denying that. That was her car and she would've been on her way home from work on the same roads the caller reported the driver being so reckless.

My dad went to law school. He knows what you do and don't want to say in front of a cop. What you should do to protect your innocence so that you don't destroy yourself in the process. As the officers were explaining the situation, my dad's mind was two steps ahead, strategizing over what he thought might happen and what he knew needed to happen in response to that, keeping my mom's best interest in mind. But before he could even complete his thought on what he predicted would happen next, my mom walked up behind him and began babbling words of incoherence. We all knew my mom was very outspoken and just as he knew she would, felt the need to defend herself. It was the last thing he wanted to happen though. The last thing he *needed* to happen. She was validating exactly what the police were there to accuse her of. She was sabotaging herself. And as soon as she started talking, they used that as an invitation to start interrogating her instead. She was criminalizing herself with every slurred word that came out of her mouth.

My dad gently pulled her aside, outside of the officers' view, and quietly asked her to stop talking. He turned back to the two officers and told them she had nothing else to say to them and that if anything needed to be discussed further, they'd want a lawyer present. My dad ended the conversation by telling them they had no evidence of her being intoxicated or under the influence while driving a vehicle. It was all circumstantial, from his perspective. Without breathalyzing her, they had no evidence to justify any further interrogation or whatever it was that was happening right there on our front porch for all of our neighbors to see.

I'm not familiar with all the legal technicalities of the situation but the officers implied they'd have someone sent over to perform the breathalyzer. They were pissed off that my dad was knowledgeable enough to stand up for her. They walked back to their cars, disgruntled, while my dad stood alone on the porch anxiously. A few minutes later, one of the officers walked back up our front porch stairs and told my dad that the highway patrolman that was on his way to our house to perform the breathalyzer had something more urgent come up that he had to attend to.

"Your wife lucked up this time," the officer hissed at my dad as he walked back down our porch stairs and opened the door to his patrol car.

As the two officers turned off their flashing emergency vehicle lights (the same lights you see when you hear sirens blaring as they fly down the highway, signaling emergency, seeking attention) and finally drove off, my dad let out a long sigh of relief himself.

"She did luck up this time", he thought to himself in agreement with the officer.

He watched their tail lights disappear and then made his way back inside. My sister and I were both in our rooms doing homework the whole time all of this was going on. Neither of us had a clue anything had happened. We wouldn't hear about this for many years either.

Even worse than my mom getting reported to the police for reckless driving on her way home from work was the huge scene those obnoxious police lights made in our little, small-town section of Lake Carolina. Like I mentioned earlier, we lived on the main road of Harborside. Anyone that lived in Harborside had to drive on the street our house sat on to get to their own house. Our street was also used for traveling to and from our neighborhood park and pool. Both of which were popular amenities on nice Summer evenings like this one. The bright flashing lights of those two cop cars parked in front of our house for close to an hour lit up our street like the 4th of July. My dad was mortified.

event two

A few months later, my dad was working at his desk from his office in our room above the garage. He was on a conference call when it was interrupted by the sounds of ringing from his cell phone. He always kept his cell phone close because my sister and I were both in after-school activities, I was new to driving with only a restricted license, and he knew his cell phone is the number we'd call if we needed anything important. When he picked up his phone, he was surprised to see that it wasn't one of us calling. It was one of the neighbors my parents had become good friends with in our time as residents of Harborside. A bit unusual, he thought. It couldn't be anything that justified interrupting his work day. An invitation to a neighborhood get together or something? He answered anyway.

As soon as he said hello, he could hear a mixture of panic and relief in our neighbor's voice on the other side of the line.

"I want to start by saying she's safe. Kellie's safe. But you need to come up here quickly."

She quickly explained that she and another woman were sitting at the entrance of Lake Carolina with my mom. She said that she was pulling into the main entrance of our neighborhood when she saw a car that appeared to have just smashed into the bushes that lined both sides of Lake Carolina's grand entryway. She and another driver in a separate car had both pulled over to see if they could help because it didn't look like the driver in the wrecked car was making any attempt to get out of their vehicle. She said something seemed wrong so they wanted to make sure everything was okay. It wasn't until they walked up to the car that they realized it was my mom's car and that she was the driver still sitting there with no sense of urgency.

"She isn't hurt but she seems unwell," the neighbor told my dad.

He knew what unwell meant which made him even more concerned and confused that she'd leave the house in the first place. It had been another one of those days she missed work and stayed in bed all day because she had taken a ridiculous amount of medication and couldn't function like a normal human. The difference this time was that she didn't usually emerge from her bedroom on those days—much less leave the house *in a car that she was driving.*

He told the neighbor he'd be right up there and thanked her for stopping to help. He rushed down the stairs of his office, jumped into his car and drove as fast as he could on that short drive up the road. A short one minute drive from our house where my mom had somehow wrecked her silver Camry into the beautifully landscaped entrance for every bystander to witness as they drove by.

When my dad got there, he thanked the two women again and told them he could take it from there so that they could be on their way. The women continued asking him if everything was okay. He reassured them that she was totally fine. He thought this might come up so he thought of a quick excuse on his drive over. He told them she had been hit hard with a stomach bug a few days prior that she was still recovering from.

"No, she seems *unwell*," they kept insisting.

"I know, but she's been *really* sick. She's had a really bad bug. I'll get

her back home now," he reassured them again, over and over.

The neighbors offered to call the cops but my dad promised he'd follow up with the subdivision and cover any costs for the damaged landscaping The last thing he wanted, the last thing she needed, was more attention from law enforcement.

As I was writing this book, my dad told me that was probably single-handedly the highest he had ever seen her. He said she had no idea where she was or what she was doing in her car as she sat there smashed into the bushes with no plans or awareness to get herself out. Apparently she was coming home from Publix - why or for what necessity on that particular day, no one knows. She certainly didn't. We would've never figured it out if it weren't for the Publix bag in her backseat. How she made it several miles up the road, shopped around Publix with other humans doing their afternoon grocery shopping, and made it almost all the way back home is almost unbelievable.

She didn't have to leave her bedroom to put her own life in danger the way we knew she already was. Now there were two confirmed incidents of her making the shocking choice to drive on the same roads being used by other innocent people despite her completely obliterate state. My mom would never intentionally hurt another soul. There was a dangerous, selfless stranger inhabiting my sweet mom's precious body.

My dad drove her home and made sure she found her way back to their bed where she'd recluse for the next few days. He took care of whatever was needed to clean up the damage she had done down the street. The way he always cleaned up after her. If it made him sad, he didn't show it. He did what he had to do to keep our ship afloat with calmness on the surface. Sometimes that meant cleaning up her mess. Some may consider that enabling behavior. I call it protecting his family.

event three

I was sitting in Spanish class one day in early 2008. The last semester of my senior year of high school. I hated being in that class and I don't think the teacher was a huge fan of me either. I have no idea why because that wasn't the normal dynamic I had with my teachers. I was a good student. I just never cared much for learning foreign languages; I much preferred math and science. Maybe I was giving off an energy that I didn't want to be there. If that was the case, I guess I can't blame her.

I'm not sure how schools operate in today's world but back in 2008, we had cell phones that we weren't allowed to use on school property. In fact, if I recall, if you got caught with your phone "on campus", it would get taken away immediately and you'd get sent to in-school detention. If a parent needed to contact their child during school hours for any reason, they called the school administrator's office and someone physically walked to whatever classroom the student was in to verbally deliver the message. It sounds so unnecessarily complicated given the world of technology we live in.

There was nothing unusual or different about this particular day. It wasn't common for people to get called out of class but it did happen every once in a while. I always wondered what warranted a student getting pulled out of class by a parent, unplanned. It had never happened to me so it piqued my curiosity any time it did happen to someone else. I can assume the reason I was pulled out of class that day was one of the more unique cases.

I was surprised to hear, "Kaitlyn, grab your stuff, they'll walk you to the front desk," when my Spanish teacher walked over to grab my attention in the middle of us working on a peer assignment.

I hadn't even heard a knock on the door over all the terrible Spanglish being exchanged around me.

"What?" I asked. I didn't know what she was talking about.

"Grab your stuff and go out to the hall. They'll walk you to the front office." She responded

Then she quickly walked off. She'd clearly already mentally moved on to other, more important things. I had no idea what was going on but I did as I was told and grabbed my stuff before walking out of the classroom.

When I got to the front office, the woman that sat behind the desk told me that my dad had called and asked for me to give him a call as soon as possible. I stood there unsure of what to do until she waved her hand, signaling my permission to leave.

If she had any other details on what my dad was needing to talk to me about, she didn't share them with me.

I walked as quickly as I could to my car. It was still early in the day, we hadn't even reached our block for lunch yet. I was confused and concerned. My dad had never called me out of school and I knew it wasn't something he would resort to unless it was absolutely necessary.

When I got to my car, I grabbed my cell phone from the glove box and dialed his number. I'll never forget what he said as soon as he picked up.

"Hey sweetie. I just wanted to let you know that your mom has been arrested. She's at the Lexington County Detention Center. I don't want you to worry but I did want you to know. I don't know who she's going to try to contact to bail her out but it's not going to be me or anyone else, if it's within my control. I've already called her parents and Lisa (her best friend) to let them know. I've asked that they also not agree to pick her up. I can't keep cleaning up after her. She's going to have to suffer the consequences of her actions this time."

He wasn't crying. He didn't sound nervous or upset. His voice was very calm, somber almost. I know he had some time to process the situation before we spoke but I was still surprised by how collected he seemed. I was in shock. I don't think the reality of what he told me sank in for several minutes after we hung up the phone. I couldn't believe my own mom had been taken into custody by the police. I was so embarrassed. Disgusted almost. I didn't think I'd ever be able to look at her the same. How could I ever take anything she said, any threat she made for punishment of my mistakes, seriously ever again?

She was always the strict parent. The one that grounded us

for what she considered unsatisfactory grades and talking back. My sister didn't really care about being grounded. She rarely got in trouble anyway. It was totally different for me. Being grounded was the ultimate punishment. It was the worst thing that could ever happen to me every time she did it. My social life meant more to me than anything else at that age.

After I got off the phone with my dad, I took a longer lunch like he suggested I do. Then I put my book bag on my back, walked back into school, and sat down at my desk in AP Physics class. Like nothing ever happened. It was the story of my life.

When I got home from cheerleading practice later that night, my dad told me the full story. My mom was driving to work that morning. He told her she shouldn't leave, that she was too messed up to be on the road. That it was a bad idea. She got defensive the way she always did—as if he was crazy for accusing her of something so sinister. She reassured him she was fine and that he was overreacting. There was nothing to worry about. She was an adult, all he could do was ask her to stay but ultimately it was her decision to go.

On her commute to work, another driver flagged her down on the interstate and somehow convinced her to pull over. This would be terrifying in any other context, being waved down by a stranger on the interstate. It sounds like the start of a true crime story. But here, the danger *was* my mom.

Once she pulled off on the shoulder of the road and rolled her window down, the other driver convinced her to hand him her keys. This was also a testament to the state of mind she was in because this was not something my mom would ever do. She was not lacking common sense and was more cautious than the average human.

With my mom's keys in hand, the man called the police.

When they got to the scene of where both vehicles were pulled over, they performed several roadside sobriety tests on my mom. All of which she failed. She was taken into custody shortly before my dad was contacted, yet again, by law enforcement. However, this time she didn't luck out. There was no escaping it. My dad wasn't around to protect her. He tried to protect her by pleading with her not to leave the house that morning but she rolled her eyes at him and left anyway. He wasn't going to be able to fix her mess this time. If this wasn't rock bottom, it was dangerously close.

8

mostly storms, rare sun

It's sad to think back to how oblivious I once was. Even at the start of my junior year of high school I didn't understand why there would be days of total normalcy and coherency followed by days my mom wouldn't once step foot outside of her bedroom. I'd ask my dad questions like:

"Why is mommy always so tired?"

"Does she not have to work today? It's Tuesday. She just started this job a week ago. Is she sick?"

"Is she not going to eat dinner with us again tonight?"

But a lot changed my junior year of high school. It became almost impossible to hide the truth from us. As a result of that, I was inevitably forced to understand the truth of what had become our new reality. It felt like one day out of the blue, it all clicked into place for me.

I finally realized that her normal days were her sober days and she only had sober days because she was running out of her prescription medications within weeks, sometimes days, of having them filled. We knew this, without a doubt, because we'd count the pills left in her newly filled but almost empty prescription bottles. She'd always hide her purse somewhere she didn't think we'd find it because that's where she kept her sacred stash of medications. Her lifeline was in that purse. It was never hard to track down the location of her purse though once she passed out. Based on very predictable behavior patterns followed by self-isolation in their bedroom, we knew we had hours if not days to count through her supply before she'd wake up again to take more.

I'm not sure why we did this, thinking back. I'm guessing it's probably fairly common behavior for the family members of an addict. In a sense, it gave us a baseline for understanding how bad of a problem she really had. To help justify the state of intoxication she was in. I remember how close I came, several times, to just flushing all those stupid pills down the toilet. But I never did it and I don't know why I never did. Did this make me an enabler too? I'm sure it wouldn't have helped the situation in any way other than a few promised, involuntary days of sobriety on her part. Back then, I would've done anything for a few extra days of sobriety with her. But I never pulled the trigger. I guess out of fear of how she'd react since her life so much depended on them.

If you walked into my parents bedroom on one of these bad days, the scene was usually fairly predictable with slight variations here and there. Sometimes she'd be in her bed, passed out with her mouth wide open, frozen in whatever position she was in when the pills metabolized and intoxicated her into an almost lifeless coma. Sometimes, she'd be sitting up with her reading glasses on, a book in hand, her head tilted so far back it looked like her neck might snap at any moment— yet she'd be fast asleep. Other times, she'd slump forward, sitting upright with the TV remote in her hand, but the pills would kick in before she could press the button to change the input, leaving nothing but blaring static filling the room.

It didn't matter what she looked like when I walked in, I always walked straight to her bedside to make sure she was still breathing. That she had a pulse.

"Phew," I'd tell myself. "She's still alive."

If she didn't seem quite so gone, I'd tap on her arm and say things like,

"Mommy. Mommy. Are you not going to get out of bed at all today?"

Sometimes my voice would wake her up just enough for her to mumble a few words. Then she'd immediately fall back asleep—unable to finish her incoherent sentence. Sometimes she wouldn't wake up at all - but she had a pulse, so she was definitely alive. I hated these days so much. I was so angry with her. I would tell her I was angry with her— not that she'd remember anything I said. It was pointless. I tried so hard to say something, *anything* to make her react. Things I know no mom would ever want to hear from their child. Things that would break their heart to know they were causing their own child so much pain.

"You're choosing pills over your own children, over your own husband."

"How can you do this to us? You are hurting us so much."

I'd say these things while she was still fast asleep, snoring with her mouth wide open, no response. My words had no impact.

There were still good days here and there. Not many of them but there were some. These were the days I learned to cling to, to soak in their entirety. I'd stay up as late as she'd let me and watch whatever movie she wanted me to because I cherished each of these hours with her so much and I knew they wouldn't last. These good days were some of the best days of my high school years. When she was good, all aspects of life felt better. These were the days I fell in love with her all over again. She was so normal, so loving, so present that I was able to forgive her for the things she did or didn't do the days prior.

The good days gave me the mom that I imagine I had before all of this started – unfortunately, so long ago I don't remember much of those times. I've seen the home videos, the pictures, our life was exactly how it was supposed to be at one point in time. I saw glimpses of the woman in those home videos on these good days. She cleaned the house, cooked dinners, gathered us in the living room for family movie nights. She challenged my dad over politics and would throw her head back in laughter over something funny I said. This mom of mine was a ray of sunshine. She had a laugh so contagious you couldn't help but throw your own head back and join in with her.

This was the mom my heart ached over when I'd wake up to find that other person living in her body once again. That familiar stranger in our house that showed up on all the bad days. An unwanted guest. When the streak of good days were over, my sadness was soon replaced with anger. Anger felt easier and less exhausting than desperation. But it was, in fact, desperation. I was desperate to not have my heart broken by my mom any longer. I was tired of feeling sorry for myself every time she let me down. I still missed her on the bad days, even when I was angry with her. But I was angry with her because I missed her so much.

I wouldn't stay mad at her once she was back. I'd forgive her quickly because that time with her was too precious and it'd be foolish to waste it. Until then, I'd look forward to the next round of good days and do my best to keep my dad company through the bad ones.

In the moment, while all of this was happening, every day seemed unpredictable. Like each day was a toss up - either good or bad. I guess that's why I continued to wake up with a little bit of hope each morning. Hoping for a good day. It's clear to see now that her behavior and the days were very much predictable. The good days were always consecutive and always preceded the series of really, really bad days. The good days were the days she was sober. And she was sober because she had no choice - she had already flown through each of her month's supplies of more controlled substances than you can possibly imagine the human body to be capable of consuming and surviving within a mere week, give or take, of having them filled.

The amount of medication she was on is difficult to put into words without sounding like I'm completely over exaggerating to make this story more interesting. It truly was shocking. I didn't understand it back then and I still don't understand it to this day. How the human body can build up such a high tolerance and be able to keep operating under those circumstances. How it could be legal to prescribe someone such copious amounts of controlled substances. Not a single medication she took was purchased illegally. She was prescribed every single one of them by licensed doctors who were each aware of everything else she was taking.

She was on both high-dose opioids and narcotics for pain from supposed fibromyalgia, benzodiazepines for anxiety, anti-psychotics and anticonvulsants for apparent bi-polar disorder, SSRIs for depression, and sedatives/hypnotics for insomnia. I never understood and often questioned all of the diagnoses she received from her doctors. From my perspective, my mom was much better off without any of these "treatments" she was receiving in excessive amounts. I use each of these drug families in a plural sense because oftentimes, she was prescribed and taking more than a single medication to treat one specific issue.

She was prescribed and abusing diazepam, nordiazepam, oxazepam, and temazepam all at once to "treat" her anxiety. All four of which are in the benzodiazepine drug family. She wasn't just taking *a* benzodiazepine for anxiety. She was taking four benzodiazepines for anxiety. A quick Google search on taking those four anxiety medications together will tell you that it is *"not recommended due to the potential for increased risks of sedation, respiratory depression, and other adverse effects, as they are all benzodiazepines with CNS-depressant effects."*

As another example, to aid her sleep even further because Ambien alone wasn't enough, Lunesta, Intermezzo and Ambien CR were also prescribed to her and would often each be filled within the same four-week period.

We'd eventually find out, years later, that her insurance company notified her two primary providers on numerous occasions of violation of her pain management contract. They reported that she was receiving Hydrocodone (Vicodin), Oxycodone (Percocet), Zolpidem (Ambien), Zolpidem ER (Ambien CR), Clonazepam (Klonopin), Triazolam (Halcion), and Chlordiazepoxide (Librium) prescriptions from three other providers at the same time her primary provider was providing Diazepam (Valium), Lunesta, Oxycodone (Percocet), Fentanyl (Duragesic), and Nucynta.

None of this was ever addressed by her providers as they

continued this grossly negligent standard of care for many years. I called one of her doctor's offices one time. It was after-hours, I remember. I was too nervous to actually speak to a human and couldn't risk someone actually picking up. But I did leave a voicemail.

"This is Kate Ingram. My mom, Kellie Ingram, is a patient of yours. I wanted yall to know that the medications yall are prescribing her are destroying our lives. Destroying our family. She is unable to function and severely abuses all of it. Please stop giving her all of this medicine."

I didn't leave a callback number so they never returned my call. I'm not sure that things would've played out any differently even if I gave them a way to contact me. I was a desperate teenager with no power, grasping at straws just trying to get my mom back.

9

rehab

2007

In August of 2007, soon after starting my senior year of high school, my dad somehow convinced my mom to go to a rehab facility for her prescription drug addiction. My hope would be that she wanted it for herself, for her husband and her children, for our family. That was unlikely though. My best guess is that multiple run-ins with law enforcement and threats of divorce are what finally got her there.

It was bad enough for me that my own mother had been arrested and taken into custody. Spending hours in the middle of a school and work day behind bars desperately waiting for someone to feel bad for her and come pick her up. I still wasn't over the arrest. I don't think I'd ever be. But now my mom was going to rehab. For drug addiction.

There was no denying she had very serious issues, problems so significant they could and would not be solved without real help. But there was something about rehab that made it feel even more official. More impossible to fix. It made me feel even more helpless. Confirmation that there was literally nothing we could do or say to make her stop. To help her help herself so that she could get better on her own. That's how bad it was. My mom was without a shadow of a doubt a drug addict.

This isn't what the life of a drug addict looks like. I was in denial. Drug addicts live on the streets. They have missing teeth and shredded clothes. They stand at traffic lights asking for money and carry the entirety of what they own in a book bag on their back. They don't have a successful career, a beautiful home, a family, children. Because if they had all of those things, a life most could only dream of, how would they ever find themselves in a position to be addicted to drugs in any form. My mom couldn't be a drug addict. She didn't fit the mold of a drug addict. Right?

But she did and she was. Rehab was proof of that. Acceptance and admittance of a problem beyond repair without professional help. What had our life become? Where did my successful, relentless, respectable mom go?

The impact this had on me is difficult to put into words. Like many aspects of this story of my life. I was embarrassed, confused, resentful, heartbroken, scared, ashamed, and a million other emotions I carried with me as I continued to live out my normal life as a 17 year old high school student. I carried this emotional toll with me to cheerleading practice and football games, while I studied for exams, went out with friends, and hostessed at a local steakhouse. When I found myself thinking about the reality of my mom sitting over there in that rehab facility, tears immediately welled in my eyes. But I'd take a deep breath, wipe those tears away as quickly as they came, and keep going about my life. If I could fool myself, I could fool everyone else. I was strong. Everything was okay.

I knew my life and what we were going through wasn't normal but the truth and reality was, at some point it became *our* normal. I couldn't understand how it got to this point. I begged her so many times to choose us. Just choose us over the pills. Please Mommy. Please just do it for us. For daddy. She never did though. She had become so selfish. When did she become so selfish? But with rehab in the picture, I had a different perspective. I was beginning to understand that she never chose us because she physically couldn't. Her agreement to go to rehab, in some ways, helped me understand why such a simple request to choose us over her pills seemed so impossible for her. The medications had a hold on her. She was far beyond dependent on them. They were crucial to her.

The silver lining was that rehab was not something she had ever agreed to in the past. From that perspective, this had to be a step in the right direction. In that regard, it gave me a sense of hope. It was terrifying that she was at a point in life of needing to be in rehab but I was hopeful. This gave me newfound hope.

Around this time, I started seeing a gastroenterologist for unidentifiable stomach issues I couldn't seem to get a handle on with dietary changes alone. I had unexplained nausea, diarrhea, cramping, loss of appetite. I'd always been healthy and active. It was unusual for me to complain about health issues like this. After many appointments for more focused assessments and testing for various allergies, intolerances, and disorders, I was ultimately diagnosed with IBS (Irritable Bowel Syndrome). Stress is a large contributor to IBS symptoms.

I think back to everything going on in my life during this

time and it seems so blatantly obvious. My body was under a ridiculous amount of mental and emotional distress. All of this had become so *normal* to me that I didn't even realize how abnormal the circumstances were. How likely it was that life itself was impacting my physical well being. It's no wonder I had stomach issues no one could figure out for so long so they labeled it IBS. The catch all for digestive issues with pre-existing mental health conditions. Life at home was extremely hard. I lived in a constant state of anxiety and fear. Maintaining that level of stress for so long eventually shows its physical impacts in other forms. For me it was very obviously in my gut.

Multiple therapists have told me that the trauma I experienced over my mom, in a sense, rewired my brain to operate in a constant state of fight or flight. My constant state of anxious, catastrophic thinking and the survival mode instinct I operate in is who I am because I was forced to think that way for so long. I've had to work really hard over the years to attempt to rewire my brain and my thinking to not default to that fight or flight response that's so deeply engraved in who I am.

Speaking of that involuntary, constant state of stressful and anxious thinking, I'll never forget the one and only time I went up to the rehab facility to visit my mom. I think it was only a few days after she walked herself into that lobby and waved us goodbye. I so vividly remember my dad cautiously preparing me to see her. He warned me, "she's not going to be herself". He explained that her body was in a major state of distress and withdrawal, even just a couple days into sobriety. My dad didn't like to worry us so I knew if he was telling me this, it meant there was a reason I needed to be briefed and not caught off guard. He was watching out for me.

I don't know if the anticipation and dread of the situation got me more worked up than I would've been had I walked in blindly or if the outcome was destined to be the same regardless. I just know I was surprised by my own weak reaction to the situation. Within mere minutes of sitting down with my mom in the visitors lobby, I had to frantically search for a bathroom. Out of nowhere, I was hit with nausea and cold sweats I couldn't bear or disregard. The whole room began spinning and I was certain I was going to lose my lunch right there in front of everyone.

I remember my high school boyfriend, Cameron, was with me that day. We had been dating for a year or so by that point. He knew both of my parents well and knew more about my mom than probably anyone else outside of our immediate family during that time. I wanted him there with me that day and I genuinely think he wanted to be there for me too. And probably even for her. The same way all of us felt about her, he too agreed that while she had her obvious issues, she was easy to love. Even he was able to see enough of her normal to form a positive, loving relationship and a certain level of closeness with her.

Cameron sat with my mom in that visitation room the whole time I was in the bathroom trying to collect myself. It had to have been over 30 minutes. He sat there with her while I sat on the floor of this grossly unfamiliar bathroom. Hyperventilating, sweating profusely and trying to talk myself out of vomiting. By this point I had learned that deep, intentional breaths usually helped me talk myself off of a ledge. I'd come to learn that a lot of the physical symptoms I'd feel in situations were driven by my current mental state. If I could calm my mind down, my body would calm down too. But that was a big

IF.

When Cameron knocked on the bathroom door to check on me, I cracked the door open hesitantly and told him I couldn't go back in there with her. The nausea had subsided but was immediately followed by overwhelming sadness and confusion. When I cracked that bathroom door, my eyes were swollen with tears and my mascara had cemented a charcoal highway down both sides of my face. I couldn't see her like that again. I wouldn't see her like that again. In so many ways, seeing her in that state of severe withdrawal was exactly what I had always envisioned a real drug addict to look like. It was exactly what it had always looked like in all the TV shows.

In hindsight, I think what happened to me at the rehab facility that day was my first of many panic attacks.

Cameron knew there was no convincing me to stay nor did he want to try to talk me into it. He respected my feelings and went back into the visitation room to say goodbye to my mom for both of us. He told her I wasn't feeling well and that we were going to leave so he could get me back home. It wasn't unusual for me to feel sick - like I said, I felt sick to my stomach fairly often those days. I hoped she understood and I knew she did. Though I have no question it still hurt her to not be able to say goodbye. It hurt me to walk away without saying goodbye. I was a coward.

On the drive home, I couldn't stop rehashing the images from that short visit with my mom. She was so nervous but not in a "nervous to see me" kind of way. She was unbelievably shaky, trembling uncontrollably, restless but not like anything I'd ever seen. It was like she physically wasn't able to sit still. A limb or one of its digits was constantly moving. Her typical very slurred speech was crystal clear but played like a cassette in fast forward. Sitting there in her presence, you could see and feel the physical pain of withdrawal in her every movement, every mannerism, every reaction and every word she spoke.

All I wanted to do was wrap my arms around her and tell her everything was going to be okay, that we were so proud of her for doing what she was doing. Reassuring her that we knew how difficult this was for her and that we appreciated what she was doing for us. But really, shouldn't it have been the other way around? I was the one who needed to be comforted. I was the one who should be comforted given the situation. This was absolutely devastating to me. But all I felt was the need to comfort her. Somehow, through all this, I had become the caretaker, the nurturer, the protector. I had to be strong for my dad and sister. They needed me more than I needed me.

For the duration of her inpatient treatment, my mom called our house numerous times throughout the day. I guess she took advantage of their designated "phone time". From what I recall my dad saying about the facility, it was pretty strict. Almost all of their belongings were confiscated from them when they walked in the door. Any personal items that could in any realm of possibility be used for substance abuse or self harm were withheld from their taking. I remember my dad telling me this because it was the first time the thought of my mom ever wanting to harm herself had ever crossed my mind. "Withdrawal can make people do things you'd never think possible" is what he told me because that's what they told him. He was equally appalled by the idea of my mom ever doing such a thing and assured me she never would. It was still terrifying to even think about or consider.

Soon after my mom admitted herself into rehab, my dad, sister, and I started attending *AA Family Group* sessions in the evenings at the church we were members of. I knew what AA stood for back then because I had gone through D.A.R.E in elementary school years prior and I had seen AA sessions referenced in a lot of TV shows. It was confusing though. My mom wasn't an alcoholic. What were we doing in sessions for family members of alcoholics? There had to be some sort of reasonable explanation though. Something brought us there after all. Something brought us to those weird and uncomfortable sessions..

I don't remember talking outside of the standard, "Hi, I'm Kate and my mom is addicted to prescription drugs".

"Hi Kate. Welcome," they all said in response.

That was all it took to be initiated into the secret society no one wanted to be a part of. A secret society most probably knew nothing about and never would. We went to a few sessions. They split the children into one group and the adults into another. I really don't recall much from these sessions other than that it was just another ridiculously unfair thing we were doing on school and work evenings while the rest of the world appeared to be living their normal lives.

Just two short weeks after my mom checked herself into that rehab facility, she was coming back home. She was nowhere near ready to leave. It was so unfortunate. Such a disappointment. Ironic, yes. We should've felt elated to have her coming back home to us. It's not so simple when you're living this reality. Her coming back home so soon wasn't a good thing and we all knew it.

My dad told us that our health insurance only covered two weeks of drug rehabilitation and we simply couldn't afford to pay out of pocket for her to continue treatment there. From what I recall, it would've cost close to a small mortgage payment each day she spent there. That outrageously unreasonable expense combined with her begging to come home is what brought her back to us. She wasn't ready, we all knew it. Two weeks couldn't possibly undo the damage she carried through those doors. Two weeks wouldn't have even scratched the surface.

When I got home from cheerleading practice late the evening before she was scheduled to be discharged, my dad asked me to join him and my sister in her bedroom. He sat us down with tears in his eyes and broke the news to us that she was coming home the next day. I'll never forget the look of defeat in his eyes as he told us he didn't expect for her to be better. He said we simply couldn't afford for her to be there any longer and we really had no choice. He hugged us both and told us he was so sorry.

After my dad collected himself, he explained to us that he had made arrangements earlier that day with each of our best friend's parents to go stay with their families for a little while.

I remember asking "Why? For how long?" This sudden shift from our normal routine made me anxious.

He replied, "As long as you want or need to stay. Each of you will have a safe and peaceful place to go home to. They have welcomed each of you to stay with them as long as you need to."

My dad then explained that the facility had standard guidelines they recommended families follow when helping patients transition back to everyday life. I can't help but wonder if those guidelines came with fine print for patients discharged long before they should've been. Based on the facility's precautions, my dad said he anticipated she would be very emotional, sick, and depressed. He didn't think she'd be suicidal but it was something he had to be prepared for in a worst case scenario. He felt it was best for us not to be around for anything that could possibly unfold. He didn't want us to see or hurt any more than we already had.

I cried when he told us this. I didn't want to leave my dad alone with her. It felt like my sister and I were the little bit of joy he had left. We respected him though and we knew he was looking out for us. He only ever did what he knew was best for us. So we did as he wished because, at the end of the day, he was the parent and we were the children. As much as it broke all three of our hearts to be split up during what was collectively the hardest thing our family had been through, it really was for the best.

That next evening, I came home after practice to grab my stuff before leaving for my best friend Emily's house. With her family is where I'd be staying for an unforeseen amount of time. I knew my dad was planning to pick my mom up sometime earlier that day so I anticipated her presence back at home when I walked in. This was another place in time I'll never forget, not for the rest of my life. Another core memory I'd say.

I had parked my hunter green Isuzu in front of our house and walked up the same stairs those police officers stood on when they followed my mom home from work that evening months prior. I remember I could hear the sound of the TV from behind the closed door of her bedroom as I walked up the staircase. I knew she was in there. My heart was unexpectedly filled with joy knowing she was back home with us where she belonged. Almost like a temporary illusion before I was reminded of the reality of what it meant for her to be back so soon.

When I walked into her bedroom, all the lights were off and

the curtains were closed shut but the TV was on so I could see she was laying in her bed. She was completely covered up in a pile of blankets - not even her face left uncovered.

I walked up beside her and said "Hey mommy," as I laid my hand on what I assumed to be her shoulder based on the silhouetted figure I could see beneath the fabrics. As soon as I made contact with her, I could feel her body shivering uncontrollably. My dad warned me of this but it still made my heart sink to my stomach. I knew she wouldn't be okay but it was different seeing it and feeling it for myself.

Without a second thought, I set my bags down on the floor beside me, took my shoes off, and curled up beside her. She was the little spoon and I was the big spoon. I couldn't see her face, but I knew she was crying. The moment I got close, I heard the soft, broken sounds of her muffled weeping—fragile and unsteady, like she was trying to hold herself together but barely could. Each quiet sob carried a weight that said more than words ever could. I felt tears begin to roll down my own face, slow and steady, blurring my vision as emotion swelled in my chest. I pulled her closer, holding her tighter like maybe, somehow, my arms could shield her from everything that hurt. The weight of the moment sank in, and in that silence, our pain spoke louder than anything either of us could say.

As I lay there beside her—the woman who brought me into this world, the very world she now seemed to be unraveling—Iam Tongi began singing "Somewhere Over the Rainbow" on *American Idol*. There was something about that song— about the tenderness in his voice, the aching hope woven into every note—that completely took my breath away. It was as if the universe had paused for a moment, letting that melody wrap around us like a warm, invisible blanket. I closed my eyes, overwhelmed by the weight of it all, and held my mom even tighter, as if I could anchor both of us through the storm. Quietly, I began to sing along—not just to the words, but to the feeling behind them. It was a lullaby of longing, of resilience, of an unspoken promise whispered into the quiet: that somewhere over the rainbow, beyond the pain and confusion, brighter days were waiting for us both.

Years later, my dad told me my mom had him stop by the pharmacy on the way home from rehab to replenish her prescription supply. I asked him why he wouldn't have told her no. It would've been simple to do, he was the one driving the car. He said, "If I didn't take her, she would've gone on her own and she was in no physical state to be on the road by herself. Taking her myself was the only option."

We all knew she wasn't ready to leave that facility, not by a long shot. It was painfully obvious that her journey was far from over, yet she was being pushed out—forced to face the world with an incomplete foundation. How sad, how frightening, it is that money holds such overwhelming power. It determines access to care, the kind of care that could have truly helped her, the kind of support she needed to rebuild herself from the inside out. That money—the absence of it, to be more precise—was the sole reason she didn't get the fair shot she deserved. It was the barrier standing between her and the only resources capable of helping her when her addiction had taken such a severe toll. She wasn't given the time, the therapy, or the healing she needed, simply because the cost of it all outweighed the value of her well-being. This haunts me.

10

the apartment

2008-2010

I don't recall much from the rest of my senior year, aside from the usual chaos that comes with being a teenager on the brink of adulthood. Senior year of high school is a bittersweet time in life. When you are unknowingly making huge decisions that will impact the rest of your life at just 18 years old.

I got acceptance letters from all four of the colleges I applied to which was a big deal for me. I had always made good grades but I had to work really hard for them. Doing well in school didn't feel like it came as easily for me like it seemed to for some. Clemson University was my top pick and I knew that's where I'd be going as soon as I opened that letter. That day, my mom snapped a picture of me holding the white acceptance letter, its bold, orange font standing out like a beacon. I couldn't help but grin, my smile so wide and cheesy it almost felt like it belonged in a commercial. With one hand awkwardly pointing to the letter—like it wasn't already glaringly obvious what the focus of the photo was—I tried to act as though I wasn't bursting with excitement. It was one of those moments where the joy of the achievement was so overwhelming that the details of the photo didn't matter as much as the sheer sense of accomplishment and pride I felt in that instant.

Clemson was always my first pick but it was also conveniently the furthest from home of those four South Carolina colleges. The distance wasn't a deal breaker for me, at least I didn't see it as a big factor in the decision. The more I think about it now, the more I wonder if it did subconsciously make it more appealing than the other three. There was no question, I knew how sad I would be to walk away and leave my family and friends behind. But it was just part of life. My first big venture into the world on my own. Just as I anticipated, I cried the whole drive home from graduation while blaring *Graduation (Friends Forever) by* Vitamin C.

Regardless of how sad I was to leave, it was the escape I needed. Whether I knew it or not back then, I needed to be able to focus on myself. At that point in my life, the problems happening at home with my mom were a huge distraction. I needed to get away. It's a good thing I was still selfish at 18 because the person I am today would've never been able to walk away so easily. And I not a single doubt in my mind, if I didn't walk away, it would've eventually destroyed me.

Right before I was officially off to start my new life in Clemson in August 2008, my parents scheduled me to have my wisdom teeth removed. Impeccable timing. I have no idea what they were thinking or what made this *the* time to do such a thing. If the decision was solely up to my mom, I would've had my doubts but I know my dad was in on it too so there was a logical explanation.

My mom took me to the procedure that day. For some reason they didn't think I needed to be put under anesthesia so they did the tooth extraction right there inside the dentist office in a chair you'd sit in for a routine cleaning. The dentist we went to was conveniently located within walking distance from our house in the neighborhood's town center. I ate a bag of Doritos before my procedure because no one told me not to. Apparently Doritos don't sit well with laughing gas and the Valium they had me take for anxiety. I threw up all over the dental hygienist in the middle of the procedure.

I tried to warn them I was going to get sick before it actually happened.

"I'm going to throw up! I'm going to throw up!" I mumbled with a mouth full of surgical equipment and a mind full of sedatives.

"Shhh. Just go back to sleep and you'll feel better. We'll be done before you know it," they reassured me.

Oh well. They can't say I didn't try to give them a heads up. They were only able to get one tooth out before they had to stop the surgery. To this day I still have those other three wisdom teeth. It was an understandably traumatizing and embarrassing experience. I don't think they do wisdom tooth extractions in dentist offices anymore. I doubt I was *the* reason but I like to think my experience was an example of why it needs to be performed in a more formal environment.

The dental assistant went out to the lobby to grab my mom after the vomiting incident. I was crying for her and wanted her there, she'd later tell me. She quickly came to my side to check on me before she began helping the office staff cleanup the mess I made. I remember her apologizing to them repeatedly and then again as we were walking out. She helped me get into her car and then took me home and set me up in their king-sized bed with all my recovery needs. It's not that my dad wasn't comforting in situations like this but his love was tough love. My mom had always been the person I instinctively turned to for comfort—the one whose presence alone could soften the blow of whatever was hurting. No one else's hug felt quite like hers, and no one else's words could ground me the way hers did.

Even as her addiction gradually took more of her from us, there were still moments—precious, fleeting ones—when she managed to show up for us in the way only she could. With a few exceptions, she could still be that soft place to land when we truly needed her, despite whatever personal battles she was fighting. And sometimes, almost miraculously, those moments of needing her would line up with the times she had already run out of her medications for the month—leaving her unintentionally sober and, in those rare windows, fully present. On those days, we got our mom back—not the version numbed by pills, but the one who knew just how to make everything feel okay, even if only for a little while.

The following week, I moved into my very first dorm room at Clemson. My mom helped us decorate as best she could to make that small cinder block dorm room feel like home. It wasn't perfect but it was much better than the uninviting, empty space we first walked into.

A few days after moving in, I started to get what felt to me like unbearable pain in the back of my mouth where my one and only removed wisdom tooth once sat. It turns out stomach acid on a fresh gum wound was a disastrous recipe for a dry socket. I had to set up an emergency appointment with a local dentist who got me cleaned up before he sent me on my way with a small dose of prescription pain medicine to take as needed.

My parents came up to visit that next weekend. I really appreciated their company because I was struggling with the distance. The tough girl that couldn't wait to get away from home had turned out to not be so tough. I was way more homesick than I ever would've imagined. My dad had to talk me into giving it more time on several occasions when I'd call him crying, begging to come home. Probably, in some ways, very similar to the calls my mom made to him from rehab almost exactly a year prior.

When my parents left later that afternoon to get back on the road and head back to Columbia, my mouth started bothering me again so I began looking for the prescription the dentist had called in for me. We searched everywhere in that dorm room. Not that there was much square footage to cover but there was not a crack or crevice left untouched. My roommate and soon to be best friend, Tracy, even joined in to help. We couldn't find that pill bottle anywhere. It was nowhere to be found.

I truly believe my mom took that pill bottle with her when they came to visit me at Clemson that day. The truth is, she was deep in the grip of addiction—a complex and devastating disease that had taken hold of her in ways we didn't fully understand at the time. The opportunity was simply too convenient for her to ignore. I don't believe for a second that she ever meant to hurt me, not intentionally. But I do believe her addiction had more power over her than she had over it. It wasn't a choice rooted in malice—it was the painful reality of someone losing a battle she never wanted to fight in the first place.

I remember telling Tracy, who I was still getting to know at the time, "I'm thinking my mom might've taken them with her. There's nowhere else that bottle could be."

She told me years later that this comment always stuck with her. That she was pretty oblivious to the depth of my mom's situation but at the time she thought it was probably very unlikely someone's mom would actually steal medicine from their own child who clearly needed it. She agrees now that, looking back, it doesn't seem so far-fetched. She was able to see for herself, over the years that followed, how sick my mom really was.

Once I found myself more settled in at Clemson with new routines, the feelings of homesickness inevitably passed. Instead of calling my parents multiple times a day, we'd go weeks without talking. My mom still reached out almost daily and left voicemails when I didn't answer. She never passed up a chance that I might actually pick up the phone. I could always tell by the sound of her voice if she'd remember leaving that voicemail or not. Sometimes her speech was so slurred I could barely understand a word she said. Sometimes I regretted not answering because her clarity was convincing of a promised normal conversation between a mom and daughter.

But I had a new life in Clemson. A new group of friends. Classes and studying kept me busy. It was easy to live in an "out of sight, out of mind" state when it came to her. In fact, those four years of college are some of the fewest memories I have of my mom's struggle with addiction. It makes me sad, thinking back on it, because my dad and sister continued to live in those dark times that overshadowed all four years of high school for me. They grew really close while I was away at college and I think it's because they really only had each other at that point. I'm just glad they still had each other.

My mom continued her cycle of getting new jobs and losing them while I was off living in my own new little world. Just as we anticipated, two weeks in rehab had zero positive impact on her addiction issues. She had picked up right where she left off. Sadly and unfortunately, because she couldn't keep a job, my parents and sister were eventually forced to move into an apartment. They just couldn't afford anything else.

I remember coming home for winter break to that apartment for the first time.

The entrance to the apartment complex was behind a Sonic fast food restaurant so when giving friends directions I'd say, "that apartment building behind the Sonic."

It was embarrassing. I was ashamed to tell people that an apartment had become our home. It's sad how selfish and genuinely oblivious I was to the depth of weight my dad was carrying to still be able to complain about an apartment I only spent a few weeks of my time in when I'd come home from college to visit on holiday breaks. My dad was doing the best he could with what he had and at that point, he didn't have much.

I do remember walking into that apartment and being pleasantly surprised with how much it still felt like home. Everything from our prior houses, for the most part, was right there. It still smelled like home. My mom was still good at giving our living space, wherever and whatever it may be, her magic touch. I appreciated that. I only went back to that apartment a few times because I didn't go home much those days. It makes me sad, to this day, to know that I escaped so much of the pain and sadness my dad and sister continued to experience over my mom throughout that time.

At some point towards the end of my sophomore year

of college, in 2010, my mom had yet another run-in with law enforcement. By that point, she had apparently started dabbling in something called "doctor shopping." I hadn't heard the term until she got caught. As I came to learn, doctor shopping—sometimes called "doc shopping"—is when someone visits multiple doctors to obtain prescriptions for controlled substances, without disclosing that they're seeing others for the same purpose. It's a tactic often used by those struggling with addiction, and it was one of the first clear signs that things had taken a much darker turn.

According to my dad, one of the doctors she attempted to "shop with" suspected suspicious behavior and reported her to the police. My mom was given the opportunity to turn herself in, which she did, to avoid prosecution. Once she did that, she was put in a pre-trial intervention (PTI) program which diverts first-time, non-violent offenders from the traditional criminal justice system into a program of supervision and services. In this program she was mandated a certain number of hours of community service as well as ongoing psychiatric care.

I actually didn't know this incident happened until several years later. That's how easy it was to separate myself from everything going on at home with my family while I was so preoccupied with the silly things I considered higher priority in my life in college. I thought my mom was volunteering at the local library because she had free time on her hands while unable to hold a job. That's what my dad told me and I never thought twice about it. I don't know why I never questioned it - it seems silly that a once strong career-driven woman would just randomly decide to start volunteering at a library, just for fun. Apparently that "volunteer work" at the library was actually community service mandated as part of her pre-trial diversion.

My dad had a quiet strength when it came to protecting us—he had this instinct for shielding us from the parts of life, and of people, that he knew would cause us pain. By this point, he must've realized that telling us the full truth would do more harm than good. The truth wouldn't fix anything—it would only deepen wounds that were already slow to heal. In some ways, the lies were a form of mercy, a way to preserve what little innocence or peace we had left. I imagine he understood that we already carried enough disappointment, enough hurt, and more than enough reasons to feel angry or ashamed of her. And maybe, in his own way, he was protecting her too—guarding what remained of her dignity, even if she couldn't do it herself. It wasn't just about sparing us. It was about holding together whatever fragile pieces were left of all of us.

A few months after the whole doctor-shopping incident, my mom completed her required community service hours and managed to land a job at a small hospital in Barnwell, South Carolina. From what we heard, she really hit it off with the hospital's CFO during the interview—something that didn't surprise any of us. First impressions had always been one of her strengths. Somehow, they were able to find a position that aligned, at least loosely, with her previous work experience. It felt like a small step forward—one of those moments where it seemed like maybe things were beginning to turn around.

That's how she found herself as the Emergency Room Supervisor. It was unexpected to say the least. It was definitely a stretch but it was what it was. There were positions she was less qualified for—like an emergency room doctor. It had a salary and by that point, any job was a good thing for her. Any job was a good thing for *them*, she and my dad both. They needed that extra income.

The summer after my sophomore year in college, I was on a quest to find an internship that somehow tied in to my mathematics major. It was a requirement as part of the eventual capstone project I'd have to complete to earn my degree. Fortunately for me, my mom was still fairly new at the hospital and hadn't been there for long enough to begin her typical and predictable patterns of self-destruction. In fact, her reputation and good standings actually helped me get an interview with the hospital's CFO and at the end of my interview, I was offered a job as his personal intern.

I don't know why it didn't occur to me at the time that this was probably not a good idea. I knew my mom and what would inevitably happen as she became more comfortable in her workplace but I guess it's all 20-20 in hindsight. It was kind of cool at first, to be able to see my mom at work. I'd gone from barely talking to her for several weeks on end while I was away in Clemson to being able to see her multiple times a day every day. Plus everyone loved her, she was easy to love, so that whole summer I was basically "Kellie's daughter". When things were going really well at the hospital, it was super obvious she was way overqualified for that job. It seemed unusual that this professional career woman from Columbia ("the big city" as they call it in the little South Carolina towns) would be working in this small town hospital in the first place. Wearing scrubs.

One day nearing the end of that summer and the end of my summer internship with the hospital, I casually walked from the little building I was working in with the other finance department staff and into the main hospital to stop in and see my mom in her office. As soon as I opened her door, my heart dropped. I saw that glazed look in her eyes from across the room. In the short amount of time I was there with her, one of the members of her staff dropped by. They needed her judgment and guidance on something but her sentences were incomprehensible. I immediately panicked but there was nothing I could do but pretend like everything was completely fine. I was used to being able to shake her arm to wake her in the middle of dinner out at a restaurant or divert attention to myself in a social setting when she was beginning to make a fool of herself. But this was different. This was her *job*.

There wasn't a chance that any single person she interacted with that day wouldn't know she was on something. She was not sober and she wasn't fooling anyone.

I texted my dad, "Mommy's messed up at work. I don't know what to do."

He replied, "There's nothing you can do sweetie. She's gotta figure this out on her own."

He was right, there was nothing I could do. I felt helpless and more embarrassed than ever before over her. This was the closest opportunity I had ever been given to a real job and I took it seriously. On top of that, I had finally seen firsthand what my mom was doing to keep losing every job had managed to get over the last six years. Even worse, these same coworkers of hers that were sure to be gossiping behind her back, judging everything about her and the situation, were also *my* coworkers. I was mortified and I was so angry.

I had made some friends that summer with some of the younger employees at the hospital. I'd go to lunch with them and we'd occasionally do some things outside of work. One day, a few weeks after the incident in her office, one of the girls asked me if everything was okay with my mom. She seemed genuinely concerned when she asked. It wasn't like she was trying to be nosey. She explained to me that she was only asking because my mom didn't seem like the same person she used to be.

She said something along the lines of, "She just seems to be sort of out of it or something."

"Oh yeah, she's definitely fine," I reassured her.

I was starting to sound like my dad covering up for her. We both knew I was lying and that she definitely wasn't fine. But she pretended to believe me and we moved on. We weren't good friends but we were friendly enough for her to recognize that I was uncomfortable and didn't want to talk about it anymore.

Another day soon after that, one of the maintenance guys I was friends with came into the office I was working out of and jokingly said, "Kate, your mom is FUCKED UP today," laughing as he continued passing by.

He said it so casually and carelessly it was clearly not something he was losing any sleep over. Much unlike myself. I had never been more ready for a summer to end.

Being in the same work environment as my mom and understanding the responsibilities of her role, I really can't fathom how often she made a fool of herself in that hospital. It wasn't just a workplace, after all. It was a hospital. There were a lot of high intensity situations. Not only that, she'd have to go to a daily board meeting and present the status of the emergency room and each patient's case, hold staff meetings, and interact regularly with executives. Seeing things from this perspective—and knowing how deeply ashamed she would've been if she'd been in her right mind—was a powerful confirmation for me of just how severe her addiction had become. It wasn't just affecting her; it had overtaken her. It had claimed her identity, shaped her actions, and silenced the version of her we once knew.

I started getting really bad waves of nausea again that summer. It had become so frequent that my parents felt like I needed to go see a doctor about it. My mom actually got me an appointment at the general medicine practice which sat right beside the hospital we worked at. My diagnosis this time around was anxiety. Well, no kidding. I wonder what that was from? That little town was so small, I can't help but wonder if that doctor I saw was well aware of the full story and knew everything about my mom. He didn't pretend to know us but I wouldn't be surprised if he did. By then, my mom had to have been the talk of the Barnwell County medical community. But that doctor was right about my anxiety. As soon as we got my anxiety under control, the nausea stopped. Who would've guessed?

My mom was fired a few months after my internship ended. I don't know if they were waiting for me to leave to make things less awkward but I could definitely see something like that being the determining factor in this small town hospital. Or maybe she had enough "good days" to get her by a few more months before they ultimately just couldn't deal with her performance issues and behavior anymore.

I'm just glad I wasn't around when it happened. It was probably for the best anyway, she was putting her life in danger in more ways than one. She was driving over an hour one-way to that hospital from the apartment each day for her commute. I don't know how she made it home some of those days after seeing her in the state she was in at work that day. I guess by this point, she had a lot of experience driving under the influence. There was a reason we never carpooled.

11

the old schoolhouse

2010-2014

In August of 2010, I was starting my junior year at Clemson while my parents found their way back to their old stomping grounds in the little town of Williston, SC. If only my mom hadn't lost her job at the hospital, she would've had a short 20 minute commute to and from work. There was no going back there though—she had burned that bridge.

Earlier that summer, my dad's dad, who we called Pawpaw Mozie, lost his very quick and aggressive battle with cancer. The timing of it was very unfortunate because he was diagnosed shortly after his wife, my grandmother, beat breast cancer. That whole period of time had to be completely brutal on her. As soon as she finished fighting for her own life, she watched her husband lose his.

I hadn't truly experienced the loss of someone close to me until Pawpaw Mozie passed away. At that age, cancer was just a word I'd occasionally heard in passing—maybe in a commercial on TV, though even those weren't as frequent or alarming as they are now. I had no personal connection to it, no reason to understand the weight it carried. I certainly didn't grasp that it could mean the end of a life. Watching my grandfather spend his final days in their home, while my heartbroken grandmother sat silently beside him, already grieving a loss that hadn't fully happened yet—those are memories etched into my mind, ones I often wish I could forget.

The sound of his breathing terrified me. The death rattle earned its name. I only knew it was that because I asked, "why does his breathing sound like that?" and that's what I was told. A chilling sound. A sound I hope to never hear again. What I remember most about this time in our lives is how much it upset my dad. It was one of the first times I saw him cry openly and unapologetically. It was as if, for the first time, he had unspoken permission to fall apart. He didn't need to hide anything—the way he was used to doing—because everyone knew the truth of what was happening with his dad.

My dad and I experienced such drastically different first losses of a parent. It's a thought process I found myself pondering fairly often after first losing my mom. Which is harder: losing a parent unexpectedly or watching them suffer before they die? I'd argue with myself that losing them unexpectedly gives you no time to prepare but watching them suffer before their inevitable death just means grieving them *while* slowly losing them. Plus, you can't possibly *prepare* for the loss of a parent even when you know it's coming. I finally settled on there being no loss of a parent any harder or any easier than another. And while the loss of my mom was "unexpected", I watched her suffer for many years before she died. I just didn't look at it like that, as suffering, while it was happening. She wasn't fighting for her life the way Pawpaw Mozie was fighting for his and if she wasn't fighting for her life because of physical sickness, she wasn't suffering. In hindsight, she was suffering and very honestly fighting for her life—just in ways my unexposed mind couldn't comprehend at 20 years old.

When my parents decided to move back to Williston, the house they bought was about half a mile up the road from Granny and Pawpaw Mozie's. It was a quaint little one story house with a neat history behind it. Prior to its reassembly in Williston, it was an old schoolhouse built on the property now belonging to Savannah River Site in Aiken, SC. In 1940, the schoolhouse was physically picked up and moved to its permanent residence in Williston where it still sits today. It was a cute house with a lot of potential. Unique characteristics like its transom windows above all of the interior doors and open floor plan gave it that authentic schoolhouse feel. But it was definitely a real fixer upper like most of the other houses that sat in that town. Unlike most of those other houses, the old schoolhouse had a fighting chance once it became the property of my mom and dad's.

My dad loved house renovation projects. He always had. He still loved houses just as much as he did back when they ran their own real estate business and would drive around for hours on Sunday afternoons house-grazing. My mom didn't care much for the physical labor of fixing up a house but she loved for him to bring her interior design dreams to life. She'd dog-ear pages from *Southern Living Magazine* and within a couple months you were almost guaranteed to find a replication of that very picture within our house. I always joke that the smell of polyurethane reminds me of my childhood—but really, it does. It's like the scent version of deja vu for me.

The original intention of their move back to Williston was to help out my newly widowed grandmother with the extensive amount of land that still belonged to her. It was too much for her to try to maintain on her own and my dad was her only son. He felt it was his responsibility to step in and help. He'd made a promise to his dad that he'd take care of Granny after he was gone and he wasn't going to back down on his word.

Unfortunately, just a few months after they moved back to Williston, my mom and Granny had a major falling out—one so intense that it left lasting scars across multiple relationships within our family. It wasn't just a simple disagreement; it was the kind of rift that quietly ripples through everyone around it, forcing people to pick sides, tiptoe around conversations, and hold onto resentments they don't quite know how to let go of.

Part of me wonders if that newly shortened physical distance between them was simply too much. They'd spent so long living at least an hour drive's distance apart, with enough space to maintain peace, that suddenly being in close proximity may have magnified the tensions that had been simmering beneath the surface for years. Sometimes, closeness doesn't heal—it exposes.

In short, some time soon after Pawpaw Mozie passed away, a piece of jewelry belonging to one of my dad's sisters went missing. For whatever reason, maybe she was just an easy target with her known reckless behavior, my mom was to blame. It seemed that in my aunt's mind, because she was an addict, it only made sense for her to also be a thief.

I don't remember all the details leading up to the big altercation but I'll never forget when it actually unfolded. Another one of those core memories. We were all at Granny's house sitting in her living room and offering our company in any attempt to distract her from the loss of her husband.

What felt like it came out of nowhere, my grandma suddenly screamed, "How would you even know if you did it?! You're so HIGH all the time, you probably wouldn't even remember."

Before I could even process what was happening, I turned to see my mom's face—ghostly pale, frozen in complete shock. I remember running over to her, grabbing her arm, and telling her, "let's go. NOW." And we both left crying.

When Granny called our house later that night to tell my dad what they believed my mom had done—that she had stolen a pair of my aunt's earrings—he calmly asked what proof they had. There wasn't any, in case you're wondering. But by then, everyone knew about my mom's struggle with substance abuse, and it made her an easy target. It didn't take much to pin something on her—especially something as painful as stealing from family. My dad knew her better than that though. She might've been an addict but that didn't change who she was as a person—as a human being. She would *never* steal from someone else and the fact that his own mother questioned his wife for doing such a thing destroyed him. It also destroyed their relationship for a very long time.

What made this whole situation even more impactful was how tight-knit we had always been with my dad's entire family. Growing up, we had huge family get-togethers on most holidays and random weekends in between. My dad had two sisters who were each married with two kids. I have so many memories with my aunts, uncles, and four cousins. We were so close that the nightly prayer I'd say out loud before bedtime for years was one I still remember:

"Thank you Jesus for Mommy and Daddy, Kaitlyn and Madeline, Granny and Pawpaw, Barbara and Papaw, Mike and Clay, Sheryl and Harold, Parker and Taylor, Janice and Tom, Tom Willis and Jessica. Thank you for my friends, family, and teachers. Please watch over us and keep us safe, healthy and happy. Amen"

It's hard to put into words how much this spat broke our family. The state of dysfunction we had entered was far beyond repair. We stopped going to holiday gatherings with my dad's side of the family and kept to ourselves from that point on. I was equally as angry about everything as my dad was and equally as hurt as my mom. It didn't matter how much my mom's addiction hurt me, it inflicted a different kind of hurt watching someone else hurt *her*. I watched my mom cry so many tears for years over things that were said to her in passing. Berating her character and accusing her of a thief took it too far. Both my grandma and aunt tried to reach out to me multiple times after everything happened but I never answered or returned their phone calls. It was much easier for me to avoid them being so far away in Clemson. It's simple to ignore a phone call when the person can't immediately drive up the street to ask why you haven't called them back. I can't imagine how difficult it was for my mom and dad to live right up the road from the family who hurt all of us so much.

About a month after my mom passed away, I got a call from my aunt. The one who speculated my mom stole her earrings. I didn't answer it, of course. If anything, I was even more resentful towards her knowing my mom left this earth with hurt in her heart over what she was accused of. My aunt was crying in her voicemail, clearly extremely upset. She said she had just found the missing earrings that she thought my mom stole from her years prior. She said she felt so guilty and would never forgive herself for hurting our family the way she did. She said she was so sorry and would understand if I couldn't find it in my heart to forgive her but she had to let me know the truth.

The truth came at no surprise to me, there was never a doubt in my mind. My mom was a genuinely good person. Addiction could take her body and her mind but it couldn't take her heart.

We did eventually make amends. I eventually found it in my heart to forgive both Granny and my aunt. It didn't feel worth it to stay angry forever. I came to understand that a lot of their bitterness toward my mom came from a place of love for my dad—and deep hurt on his behalf.

I also recognized that I was in a unique position: I knew my mom well enough to be certain she would never do something like that. But for those who didn't know her the way I did, it must've been hard to make sense of the changes in her behavior as she battled the darkest parts of her addiction. Looking back, I can better understand their perspective. From where they stood, she didn't seem like the same person anymore. And when someone you love starts to feel like a stranger, it becomes easier—almost instinctive—to blame the stranger, not the person you used to know.

In May of 2012, I graduated from Clemson University with a Bachelors of Science in Mathematical Sciences. My mom got these beautiful graduation announcements printed out to send to family and friends. She was so proud of me. My whole family came to my graduation and we ate at Olive Garden afterwards to celebrate. A few months later, my mom surprised me with my diploma professionally framed with accents of the school's colors, orange and purple, in the photo mats. She always did thoughtful acts like this. Gifts I may not appreciate as much in the moment but would obviously mean so much to me once I had a more mature understanding of the important things in life. The things worth celebrating and being proud of. The accomplishments worth framing and hanging on a wall.

Right after college graduation I got a job at an accounting firm in Columbia, SC. Just a short 20 minute drive from where it all started in the green house. This firm was by no means a place I planned to stay but it was a step in the right direction. I worked there for about a year before I was accepted into an entry level training program to begin my career in IT at the company I still work for today. I had no money to my name as a newly working professional but my parents helped me get on my feet, helped make my new apartment a home, and were there for me when I needed them—just as parents should be. My mom was usually over-medicated when they'd show up, but she was there and that mattered. I was only about an hour drive away from their house in Williston at this point so I saw my parents more often, especially on the weekends.

By this age, in my early 20s, I was experiencing a slight shift in priorities. I still felt a strong pull to my social life and spending time with friends but my empathetic side really beginning to show itself. I was becoming more aware of my dad's feelings and I could pick up on his intensifying depression. With Madeline ad me both out of the house, his primary companions were their two dogs. My mom was spending most of her time isolated in their bedroom by this point with the exception of the rare good days here and there. Over time, my mom reached out less and less and I knew what that meant. Things were just continuing to get worse. Somehow, despite all the run-ins with law enforcement and notifications from her health insurance to providers, she seemed to have gained access to even more medication. The bad days and good days were becoming less and less proportional. There were now way more bad days than good days.

In early 2014, I went through a breakup and heartbreak so devastating it completely unraveled me. It was a sadness I'd never known—deep, raw, and all-consuming. I remember getting into my car without even thinking and driving straight to my parents' house in Williston, as if something in me instinctively knew where I needed to be. As soon as I pulled into their gravel driveway behind the house, I rushed through the backyard and opened the back door without hesitation. I already knew exactly where to find my mom. And honestly, I didn't care what state she was in—whether she was sober or not didn't matter to me at that moment. Sometimes, when your heart is completely shattered, the only thing that can hold it together, even briefly, is your mom.

I dropped my bags, walked straight into their bedroom, crawled under the covers beside her, and let myself fall apart. I cried until I couldn't anymore, tucked into her arms like I had been as a child. She held me tightly and whispered promises that everything was going to be okay. I didn't believe her—not then. In that moment, happiness felt impossible, unreachable. But I didn't need truth or hope. I just needed her.

As I lay there, I felt warm tears land on my cheeks—tears that weren't my own. But I wasn't surprised. My mom had always cried when I cried, as though the invisible cord that once connected us had never really been severed. She felt my pain as if it were her own. Now that I'm a mother myself, I finally understand what that kind of love feels like—the kind that aches when your child aches, the kind that reaches for them even in their darkest moments, no matter what.

My mom made a conscious effort to check in on me more after I went through that really hard breakup. She asked if she could come up to my apartment in Columbia one weekend soon after I showed up at her bedside and cried in her arms. She said she wanted to have a girls weekend. I was a little anxious for it because I didn't really know what to expect from her but I figured if she was reaching out and initiating plans, that probably meant she was fine. Sadly, it also meant she had probably flown through all of her prescriptions and had no other choice but to be fine. But I chose to ignore that reality.

To my surprise, she was really good that whole weekend. It felt so good to have her there with me. To have *her* there. My mom always catered to me the way I now cater to my daughter. She'd wait on me hand and foot because that's just what made her happy. I think it gave her little glimpses of my childhood again. She came up that Friday after I got off work and stayed the whole weekend with me. She cooked us dinner each night. We watched Lifetime movies all day Saturday, and she cleaned around my apartment that Sunday while I got some work done. She asked if she could stay that Sunday night and told me she'd just leave that next morning when I left for work. I was fine with it, I was genuinely enjoying her company. I knew I'd miss her a lot when I came back to that empty apartment Monday evening.

We had the best time that weekend and I know she really appreciated it too. She loved being with me and Madeline both but she and I had grown especially close in the little bits of time we got to spend together on her good days. We had so many things in common that I was able to see for myself the older I got. Similar styles, interests, beliefs. There was so much potential for us to be the very best of friends.

I left for work before her that Monday morning.

She gave me a big hug and told me, the way she always did, "I'm so proud of you. Hold your head up sweetie. I'll call you later this week. I love you."

When I got home from work later that evening, I found a sticky note on my kitchen table from her.

We need to do girls weekends more often. I had the best time with you. Call me anytime you need me, sweetie, and I'll come up. I love you so much. I'm so proud of you.

-Mommy

2014 was a hard year in general for our family. My mom's dad, Papaw John, was diagnosed with lung cancer that summer as well and almost immediately began chemo treatments. My mom's mom, Barbara, tried to take care of him at their home on her own but it was just too much for her. Though my mom didn't like the idea, Barbara decided it was best for his well-being and for her own mental health to get my granddad into an assisted living facility right up the road from both of their houses in Williston. The plan was for him to be up there for long enough to get his treatment completed. At least there, he'd have hands-on, professional care 24/7. My mom went up to that facility every single day of his time there and spent hours by his bedside. My last picture with Papaw John was hugging him from his bed inside that room.

My mom got a call one late November night from one of the nurses at the facility. She extended her sincerest apologies and told my mom that when they walked in to do their nightly visit with Papaw, to check his vitals and such, he was unresponsive. We were all in shock. In disbelief, really. He was scheduled to be going back home within the coming days because he appeared to be showing such positive signs of improvement from his treatments. This broke my mom's entire heart in two. Much like my dad, her dad meant everything in the world to her. She was completely devastated.

Thanksgiving and Christmas in 2014 were both sad holidays. It's unusual when a prominent presence in your life just disappears in the blink of an eye. Their void is loud and haunting. That's what the rest of 2014 felt like—especially with two of the year's biggest holidays and reasons for gathering as a family following shortly after his loss. My mom cried a lot. I was around to see a lot of it because I was around for the holidays. When I'd go back to my apartment in Columbia between visits, I barely ever heard from her. It was such a stark difference from the mom I knew she was—deep down in there somewhere. But when she didn't try to call, didn't have any interest in reaching out or catching up, I always knew what that meant. The tremendous loss of her father was another reason to bury herself in her bedroom and find comfort in the places she always knew she could rely on—the bottom of those pill bottles.

My mom and I took our last picture together on Christmas Eve of 2014. I remember us having Uncle Mike snap "candid" pictures of us that weren't really candid—we were pretending to be laughing in the moment. I remember my mom wasn't quite herself that day but she also wasn't totally gone. If I had to pick a specific kind of bad day for my mom, the kind of bad day she had that Christmas Eve would've been my preference. Not totally there but also there enough to be physically there. At least we got to see her and be around her that Christmas Eve.

ID

Part Two

1966-2002

12

best all around & most likely to succeed

1966-1995

My parents were in their early 20s when they had me and my younger sister, Madeline. I can't fathom having two children by 26. I was so self-absorbed and irresponsible at that age. Children force you to be selfless and responsible. I guess my parents became both of those much earlier in life than me. We gave them no choice.

My mom, Kellie, and my dad, Mark, were both born in 1966. My dad was just two months older than my mom. They would eventually both grow up in the small, one stoplight town of Williston, South Carolina—population 2,722 in 1960 for reference. I say they both *eventually* grew up in Williston because my mom was actually born in a small mountain town one state over in Western North Carolina. That town was called Canton. Her family moved to Williston for my granddad's job when she was in middle school, circa 1979. Everything I've heard about their move away from Canton tells me it was extremely hard for her and her family. My grandparents' roots ran deep in that little mountain town. It would always be a part of her. She was always proud to be from North Carolina.

I carry a handful of cherished memories from my childhood from our visits to Canton. My mom adored that town—she was fully immersed in its rhythm, its people, and its quiet charm. She wanted us to love it the way she did, and she went out of her way to make sure we understood what it meant to her, hoping it would mean something to us, too.

We often visited my great-grandparents at their little mountain ranch, especially on sunny days when the air felt lighter. I distinctly remember the smell of the paper mill we'd pass when we were getting close to their house. That was always the point in the drive when I no longer had to ask, "are we almost there?" The smell answered that question for me. Summer cookouts were a tradition at my great-grandparents' house—carefree afternoons filled with grilled food, sticky fingers, and slices of watermelon, which my mom, sister, and I ate while wearing matching watermelon-print dresses she'd picked out just for the occasion.

We'd laugh until our bellies ached, playing with our third cousin Caleb, while our parents took turns pushing us on a tire swing that hung from the old oak tree, its roots buried deep in the backyard soil like the generations that came before us. We made up a silly song once that we'd always sing when we were together those summers.

"Down yonder where the green grass grows, my mama and my papa were sippin' on some Pepsi, ya know?"

The song made no sense to us then either. But it stuck with us year after year, summer after summer. A familiar melody from the good ole days.

The air in Canton always smelled different—sweeter, fresher. The kind of air that made you instinctively roll your window down just to be able to take it all in.

My mom and dad first met in middle school—just kids trying to figure themselves out, unaware that their paths would eventually become so deeply intertwined. As the years passed, they found themselves in the same circle of friends, and by their junior year of high school, a relationship had quietly blossomed between them. It started the way so many young love stories do—with shared glances, late-night phone calls, and that electric sense of something new and exciting.

My mom was a cheerleader, bold and full of life, known for her big personality and an effortless ability to command a room. She had a party girl reputation, but there was more to her than that. Her classmates admired her enough to vote her "Best All Around" in their senior superlatives—a reflection of how loved and well-rounded she truly was, even back then. My dad, on the other hand, was quieter and more reserved. He played drums in the band, studied hard, and earned the title of salutatorian through his sheer determination and focus. His classmates recognized his drive and potential, naming him "Most Likely to Succeed." Where my mom radiated spontaneity and charisma, my dad exuded stability and ambition.

They couldn't have been more different—my mom was the heartbeat of the crowd, my dad the the calm in the chaos. And yet, that contrast seemed to work for them. Somehow, their differences became the glue that held them together. Their love story had all the hallmarks of classic high school sweethearts: young love, strong emotions, and a belief that together they could take on the world. And for a while, they did.

In 1984, my parents graduated from Williston Elko High School. Both with plans for college just around the corner. My dad always hoped to become an architect which is what drew him to Clemson University to begin his studies there in architecture. This meant not only leaving his small town but also the love of his life behind. My mom, on the other hand, didn't want to venture far from home. Not that Clemson was across the country or anything. But when you grow up in a town like Williston, moving several hours away feels like you've left for another country. While my dad committed to Clemson that Fall, my mom decided to stay closer by and began working on her accounting degree at the University of South Carolina (USC)'s Aiken campus. That particular USC campus was just a short 30 minute drive from her family home back in Williston. She was able to get the best of both worlds this way—her parents right up the road and a new sense of freedom living on her own. The only thing missing was my dad. I, too, had a high school sweetheart. I know how heartbreaking and overwhelming this was for them.

I think it's fair to say that most high school sweethearts struggle to survive the shift that comes with going to separate colleges. Long distance brings with it a new kind of weight— one that often proves too heavy for young love to carry. College marks the beginning of a completely new chapter, one where you begin evolving into a version of yourself you've never known before. In high school, your world feels small—shaped by your town's borders and the familiar faces that fill its hallways. But when you step outside of that bubble, your world stretches. You're exposed to new ideas, new people, and new possibilities. You start to question everything you thought you knew, including the love you left behind.

It's something I think about when I see couples who I know never left their hometown. I wonder if they ever think about what—or who—might be waiting for them beyond those familiar streets. If maybe, just maybe, the person truly meant for them is living a life somewhere they'll never cross paths with. A soulmate lost to distance and circumstance. Not in this lifetime, at least.

My parents wrote letters back and forth to each other throughout that first year of college they spent apart. My mom kept every single one of those letters stashed in a shoe box. I still have that shoe box. I've also read a few of those letters. There was no question that they were madly in love and longed to be together again. You could feel the ache in their hearts in the words they shared in those letters. It made sense why my dad decided to come back home to her after that first year, leaving Clemson and enrolling at the University of South Carolina's Aiken campus and back to where he belonged—at my mom's side. He couldn't bear the thought of losing her, so he did what he knew he had to do to hold on. Walking away from the education he'd dreamed of at Clemson was no small sacrifice—it was a future he'd worked hard for, one he truly wanted. But in the end, she meant more to him than any degree ever could. She was his everything, and that was the choice he made.

In December of 1987, my dad graduated a semester early with a Bachelors of Science in Political Science. My mom followed shortly thereafter, graduating right on time herself, with her own Bachelors of Science in Accounting that May of 1988. My mom got a job offer at a small accounting firm right after graduation. While she began her career there, my dad worked part time at his parents' car lot and continued studying for the

LSAT with ambitious plans to begin his journey into law school in the Fall.

My parents didn't waste any time—marrying that June, in the summer heat of 1988, at the First Baptist Church of Williston. The sanctuary was filled with family, friends, and the soft hum of small-town chatter. My mom's bridesmaids wore dusty rose dresses, their puffed sleeves puffier than they needed to be, perfectly matching the sleeves of her own gown. Her hair was styled in a voluminous, permed pixie cut—bold, bouncy, and very much in line with the trends of the late '80s. There was a charm to it all—classically sweet. Big hair, bigger sleeves, and the biggest smiles you've ever seen. It was a picture-perfect moment for two kids just beginning to build a life they had no idea would be filled with so many twists, turns, and everything in between. But that day, in that church, all they knew was love—and that was enough.

Their reception was a short walk over from the sanctuary to the church banquet hall where everyone gathered to celebrate the newlyweds, Mr. and Mrs. Mark and Kellie Ingram. They drove off in a silver Buick Park Avenue with "Just Married" painted on the back that their friends decorated on their behalf. Cans dangled from rope tied to each of the side mirrors to create a loud exit as they clanged against the pavement for their departure down Main Street. Their first car ride as husband and wife. I still have a small, off-white book cloth photo album that was given to them as a wedding keepsake. It has *Our Wedding* embroidered on its cover with picture sleeves full of moments captured that day. Most of the faces that stood beside them at the altar are the same faces I grew to love and cherish throughout my own life. Everything about that day was small town, simple, and sweet—much like the two of them.

Their first year of marriage was full of love and figuring out their new life together. My dad ended up scoring well on the LSAT and got accepted into the University of South Carolina's School of Law just as he hoped. My mom's first job at that small accounting firm gave them just enough income to barely scrape by that first year.

They found out they were pregnant with me right after their first wedding anniversary. I was born in March of 1990 during my dad's second year of law school. I've heard many stories about the long, early morning and late night drives to and from law school classes with a newborn at home. He still jokes that those drives gave him some of the only sleep he was offered during that time—though I think there was probably some scary truth to those stories. Long before I knew it, before I knew him, my dad had this effortless strength about him—still almost impossible for me to understand. He's always seemed to do what he has to do to make things work.

My younger sister, Madeline, came along two short years after me. She was born very premature at 30 weeks. My parents always described her fragile size as easily being able to fit inside a small men's shoe box. When they were finally able to welcome her home from her long stint in the NICU a few months later, she was hooked up to all sorts of medical equipment. Heart monitors, oxygen, a feeding tube—she required very attentive care.

It was after bringing my sister home that they realized that staying in their hometown close to their own parents, our grandparents, was the best thing for them in those early years. My dad was still spending the majority of his waking hours either in or driving to and from law school classes while my mom continued working as the breadwinner of the family.

They needed all the extra help they could get with young kids. Fortunately for them, both sets of grandparents were open arms to help out where they could. They were familiar with the hardships of trying to get on your feet while raising a family.

13

my grandparents

My mom's parents and my dad's parents couldn't have been more different. Different upbringings, different lifestyles, different personalities, different morals and ethics. Just entirely different sets of humans. I picked up on that from a very young age. I had such strikingly different relationships with each set of grandparents too. It's like, even at the very young age I was, I could sense how different they were and therefore acted and bonded with them in completely different ways.

I tended to feel like I could be myself and act more silly at Barbara and Papaw John's house. In my mind, I could get away with more because there were less invisible boundaries there. As long as I took my shoes off before I even thought about opening the front door, that was enough to keep Barbara happy. On the other hand, at Granny and Pawpaw's there was more structure and discipline. I knew I had to be a better listener at their house because Granny wasn't against putting us in timeout. She'd threaten a whoopin but I never had a problem reminding her that mommy and daddy didn't spank us. She never appreciated my talking back either. We loved her though. She just had a tougher kind of love than Barbara. Granny didn't tolerate bad behavior or disrespect in her house. You can't fault a woman for commanding respect.

My mom's parents were what I'd consider now to be a little rough around the edges. I didn't see it as such back then but now that I've seen the world through more mature eyes, I think that's an accurate way to describe them. Especially if you compare them to my dad's parents. Her mom and dad were Barbara and John Burch. I called Barbara by her first name ("Barbara") and John "Papaw John". We decided to proceed Papaw with "John" because my other granddad was "Pawpaw" and the two—Papaw and Pawpaw—sounded exactly the same from the mouth of a young child. The only clear differentiation was the name that followed. So "Papaw John" it was. For Barbara, she cringed at the idea of being a grandma. She said she wasn't old enough to be a grandma. She really wasn't—she was just 42 when I was born. Exactly 20 years older than my mom. Because she was so adverse to the idea, she didn't want constant reminders of the unavoidable reality of it either. No "Mamaw", "Grandpa", "Meemaw". Absolutely none of that. Just Barbara.

Barbara and Papaw John were both born and raised in Canton, North Carolina. They brought their strong western North Carolinian "mountain" accents with them to South Carolina when they picked up and moved when my mom was in middle school. They were both chain smokers for most of my mom's life so their house and everything and everyone belonging to it smelled like smoke. When I think of secondhand smoke, I think of that house of theirs in Williston—with its once white popcorn ceilings yellowing by the time I came along from the years of cigarette smoke they sheltered. The smell of their house was a unique but familiar, homely smell to me as a child. Kind of like that of a bowling alley back then—but a more clean, lived in version of that.

Barbara and Papaw John were two very different breeds of human themselves. I always said Barbara was my "favorite grandparent". My mom always asked me not to say that out loud. She said I could think it but I shouldn't say it. She told me it would hurt others' feelings and that I shouldn't voice those kinds of feelings. I respected her wishes but I know Barbara knew how I felt. I made sure she knew. My mom definitely did too. Barbara was always the most patient with me—it felt like she genuinely enjoyed my company. Like she wasn't just doing my parents a favor by keeping me. At least she never made it seem that way to me. I remember going to their house and sitting in Barbara's lap rocking with her for hours in her appointed rocking chair. She'd chain smoke the whole time— her ash tray and Marlboro cigarettes always within arm's reach of where we sat.

Barbara's chair always sat diagonally across from Papaw John's rocking chair, tucked into opposite corners of their living room. They were near each other, but with just enough space in between—close, yet distant. They were often short with one another, their tempers quick to spark. You could sense in their back-and-forth that they were probably one of those couples who had only ever known each other in their little town. It felt like maybe they weren't each other's true soulmates—maybe those people were out there somewhere else—but Canton tied them together, and that's the life they lived. Thank God for that, because it gave me my mom—and it gave me Barbara. Rocking together in that chair of hers is where I learned how to whistle and snap my fingers. Two impressive skills I was proud to show off at such a young age. Not many other three-year-olds knew how to whistle and snap.

Barbara was a quirky woman. She had a unique and silly personality. I guess her quirkiness was fitting with wanting her own grandchildren to call her by her first name. In her younger adult life, she was a beautiful woman. The yellow, smoke tinted photographs from that time attest to her beauty. Tan, thin, big hair. I don't think I've seen a single picture of her without cigarette in hand. As she got older, the nicotine began to catch up with her appearance. She always had dark circles under her eyes—it was a distinctive feature of hers that stood out to me. She was a well-kept woman though. She cared about how she looked. She was just no longer the tan 1960s barbie I saw in pictures by the time we came around. She did eventually stop smoking when I was much older. I don't remember exactly when or why but that familiar smell in their house faded slowly with the passing years.

My mom was the oldest of Barbara and Papaw John's three children. She had two younger brothers, my uncles, Mike and Clay. Both Uncle Mike and Uncle Clay were hot topics in the little town of Williston in the 1980s. They both came out as homosexual at some point in their early twenties—Uncle Mike a year or so before Uncle Clay. From the stories I've heard, it surprised a lot of my people. Except for my mom. She claimed she wasn't oblivious. The interests my uncles had were evident to her to be unlike any other boys she knew growing up. They liked playing dolls with her and organizing little plays to perform for their family in the living room. My mom told me Papaw John had a really hard time processing this news and had an even harder time accepting it—being the southern mountain man he was. Barbara wasn't so fond of the idea either, as much as it killed her not to applaud their vulnerability and strength and welcome them with open arms.

This news really shook things up. Not just in their one story, smokey, brick ranch but the entire town of Williston had also gotten word of it before long. Secrets don't keep in small towns like that. I do applaud their bravery though. Even in today's world, people live their lives in secret due to fear of rejection. My Uncle Mike told me that while my mom wasn't completely welcoming of the idea at first, she was the first to come back with a change of heart. The first to tell him she still loved him and that would never change. She was also the first to be willing to try to accept them for who they were. Hearing that didn't surprise me one bit. My mom loved everyone. Her one love heart and mindset was also years ahead of its time.

Growing up with Barbara apparently had it's twists and turns. I heard a story once about something that happened on my mom's 13th birthday. She had one of her good friends over to hang out at their house. When her friend got there, my mom told her to follow her back to her room. Once they were in secrecy and behind closed doors, my mom took out a cup of what appeared to be orange juice to show her friend.

"Look what mama gave me this morning for my birthday."

"Looks like orange juice," her friend said.

"It's a screwdriver. Orange juice with vodka. Mama wanted me to have my first drink with her."

My mom's friend was shocked. Growing up in a Baptist household herself, they were never around alcohol. Much less a parent encouraging their 13 year old child to drink. At 13, my mom probably thought she had the coolest mom in town. All I know is my mom was not that mom to me. She was quite the opposite. I guess at some point, she realized that giving your child alcohol was not only uncool, it was totally irresponsible. I'm willing to bet my mom made a promise to herself she'd never be that kind of mom.

Barbara had a difficult upbringing herself. Her mom, my great grandmother, Inez Dixon, was an alcoholic and drug addict. She worked as an in-home nurse for many years and was caught stealing prescription medications from her patients on numerous occasions. She also attempted to commit suicide one day when Barbara and her siblings were at home alone with her. Barbara, her sister, and two brothers were stuck on the other side of the locked door. Their little hands pounding and lungs screaming as they begged her not to leave them. Just four young children pleading with their mom not to take her own life.

I was too young to really understand the person Barbara was during the time I had with her. She was fun to be around and she didn't seem to take life too seriously which was the ideal grandparent in a child's eyes. I learned later in life that she had a severe case of OCD. This made sense of a lot of things for me. It explained why she was so particular about her house. Everything had a very specific and correct place. Shoes came off before even opening the front door. If you accidentally forgot, it was a very big problem. Not that she would be mean about it. But she would genuinely panic. She'd watch her living room carpet like a hawk. There couldn't be a speck of dirt, grass, or food crumbs on her watch. If there was, it was gone before it even hit the ground. And she always had the same water cup that sat by the kitchen sink. She'd neatly and carefully take a sip from her cup and then delicately place it back on a carefully folded paper towel. That piece of paper towel had been pulled from the roll at the start of that morning. That same piece of paper towel was used throughout the day to dab any perspiration that escaped the sip from her cup and was also used as a cup holder to defend against any threatening water rings on her yellow laminate counter-tops. She was a predictable woman, that Barbara.

My granddad, Papaw John, was your stereotypical southern cowboy of a man. Gruff and tough. If he felt excitement, he never really showed it. In the years I knew him, he always had a very prominent mustache and a comb over. He was a very handsome man in his prime. He played football for the Air Force for a few years. Something I always thought was cool was that his brother, my great Uncle Jim, played football for Duke and the Washington Redskins. Those Burch men were football men. Papaw John loved drinking cold beer—Coors Light, deer hunting, and watching football from his appointed spot in his lazy boy recliner. He was a die hard USC fan so he loved giving me a hard time when his team would play Clemson. Clemson and the University of South Carolina (USC) are the state of South Carolina's two biggest universities. They're also the state's two biggest rivals. The last Christmas present I gave Papaw John was a framed picture of Clemson's Death Valley football stadium. It was a cheap frame from the Dollar Store with a picture I printed out from my desk printer. It was intended to be a joke and we both got a good kick out of it. But that gag gift sat right there on the side table beside his chair in the living room until the day he died. He was a gruff man but he had a heart of gold. He loved my mom more than anything.

She was his baby girl. He always called her "darlin".

And then you have the Ingram's. My dad's parents were a totally different species from the Burch's. Rosemary and Mozie Ingram. His parents, who I called Granny and Pawpaw Mozie, were more of your stereotypical small town maw and paw. They were both extremely conservative in their social and political views. They were also very active members of the First Baptist Church of Williston. They owned a used car lot for many years which they ran from a small piece of the huge acreage they owned in Williston. They always called those 130 acres of land "the farm." To me, it felt like more than a farm and more like they owned most of the town of Williston.

Granny and Pawpaw Mozie were frequent movers throughout the town of Williston. Much like our family but on a smaller scale and contained within the Williston town limits. They were loyalists to Williston, I suppose. My dad lived a similar childhood to mine in that regard—he didn't have a single "childhood home" because they were always picking up and moving to the next house a few miles down the road. It must be genetic—that wanting to move constantly. I'm kind of hoping I didn't get that gene. Only time will tell I guess.

Granny was always a very petite woman but her small frame didn't mean she couldn't pack a punch. My dad said she was the sweetest woman, the sweetest mom, when he was growing up. That was under one condition, you didn't mess with her family. She was very strong-willed and fiercely protective of her family—especially of my dad. He was her youngest child and her only son. Her baby.

I'm not sure what the relationship was like between her and my mom before I was old enough to acknowledge it and care enough to think twice about it. What I do know is that by the time I was in middle school, the dynamic between them had approached toxic territory. I didn't understand it for a very long time—another one of those truths that uncovered itself as I wrote this book. I never understood why my mom was so upset after being around Granny. How we'd reached the point of leaving almost every family gathering with my mom in tears as she whispered to my dad about the hurtful things Granny had said to her. But as I got older, as I really began to understand what was happening beneath the surface, it began to make more sense.

Despite the rocky relationship she had with Granny, my mom always seemed to hold a unique and precious place in Pawpaw Mozie's heart. It was as if he saw her clearly—the best parts of her—and chose to focus on those, quietly accepting the rest in a way that others often struggled to do. Pawpaw Mozie was a man of few words, soft-spoken and reserved, but when he did speak, his voice carried a gentle kindness that stuck with you. He was such a sweet man. I always felt comfort in his presence. He was a tinkerer, much like my dad—always fixing, building, or fiddling with something around the house. Half the time, what he was working on wasn't even broken. He just needed a project, something to keep his hands busy and his mind engaged. Sitting still never suited him.

His full name was Mozie Ingram. No middle name—just Mozie. Simple and unique, just like him. Everyone knew them as Mozie and Rosie—and their names flowed together like they were meant to be said as a pair. The way they fit, the way they moved through life together, made their love feel inevitable. There was never any doubt in anyone's mind that they belonged to one another. You could feel how much they enjoyed each other's company when you were around them.

They did everything together until the day my PawPaw Mozie died. Their souls were made for each other.

My parents came from vastly different worlds, shaped by experiences that couldn't have been more opposite. As I've grown older—and especially through the lens of therapy—I've come to deeply understand just how profoundly our early environments influence who we become. Childhood experiences form the bedrock of how we navigate life: our capacity to cope with challenges, how we express emotion, whether we learn to rely on ourselves or depend on others. Therapy has taught me that these patterns are not just abstract ideas—they're real, powerful forces. And I've seen it firsthand in the lives of my own parents.

My mom and dad faced life through very different lenses, each one tinted by the values, traumas, and expectations of the homes they were raised in. Their differences weren't just personality traits; they were reflections of how they were shaped by their families, their communities, and the emotional resources (or lack thereof) they were given. I now realize that understanding someone's childhood is often the clearest way to understand the adult they become.

14

the house in tennessee

1995-1999

In 1995, my parents decided to take a big chance and a bold step for them—venturing out of the little town of Williston. By 1995, I'd already spent five years of my life in that little town. My entire world and everything I knew was there. My parents didn't want that for us though. They loved Williston but they wanted us to know more, to see more, to do more. They wanted us to be a part of something bigger. To do bigger things. They wanted us to experience more than what was within that one stoplight town. So they picked up and moved our little family of four to a town right outside of Nashville, Tennessee. That town was called Franklin.

It was a pretty little town even back then. It's appeal was that it was far enough out of the city to avoid the hustle and bustle of tourists that Nashville brought to that area yet still conveniently close to Music City. When we moved to Franklin, we lived in a newly developed, all-brick community called Polk

Place. It was a quintessential all-American neighborhood with sidewalks, friendly neighbors, and tranquil shade trees. That two story house in Polk Place felt huge in comparison to the tiny one-story brick ranch we left behind in Williston. In Polk Place, we had a fairly large lot—nothing huge, we were in a suburban area of town. But it was big enough for us. We had enough space to run around in our fenced in backyard with a custom wooden play set my dad built just a few months after we were all settled in. The front yard was a good size too. That driveway is where I first learned to ride a bike—with and without training wheels.

Looking back, I'd say these were probably some of the best days, if not best years, of our family's life together. My parents both had successful careers, Madeline and I were both in elementary school in a great school district, we had two beautiful Boxer dogs (Jack and Sam), and our life was just a happy place to be. We'd go to a community park on Sunday evenings with our dogs and have dinner over a family picnic in one of the open fields in the park after playing on the playground. You could see in the smiles across all of our faces from pictures at this park that we were living the American Dream.

In Tennessee, I danced for Nashville City Ballet. This was a big change for me because the studio I danced for back in South Carolina, the only studio within driving distance of Williston, was way more casual and less disciplined. There was no sense of structure like the big ballet school in Nashville. We had to wear very specific hunter green leotards, tights of a specific shade of pink, and our ballet shoes had to be purchased directly from the school itself. My hair also had to be in a slicked back bun for every class. I never enjoyed that. Thanks to ballet, I became very familiar with bobby pins and hairspray. Wisps and loose, dangling hairs were absolutely not acceptable.

I remember my mom and I would sing Celene Dion songs at the top of our lungs on our drives to and from dance class. After class, we'd stop at a local bakery in downtown Franklin and get tea cakes and lemonade for the drive home. My mom loved watching me dance and she never missed a class.

My sister expressed interest in gymnastics at some point while we were living in Tennessee so my parents signed me up for that too so that she wouldn't have to go at it alone. I still laugh when I see pictures of myself, that my parents felt were worthy of paying for and printing in mass volumes, posing for the photographer they brought in to the gym for each of the gymnasts. It was definitely not the sport for me. I looked so awkward and uncomfortable doing those gymnastics poses.

Home videos were really big in the 1990s so a lot of the video footage I've seen from over the years came from that period of time in our lives—the years we lived in Tennessee. What always stood out to me watching those home videos was how fortunate our Christmases were. We were too young to even realize it. I'll never be able to forgive myself for the way I watched myself act one of those Christmases. In the video, my mom excitedly handed me a wrapped gift so my energy was feeding off of hers. Seeing her so excited meant it was something worth being excited over myself. When I unwrapped the present, I immediately pouted at the Pocahontas music box sitting in front of me. I guess it's not what I wanted and I let it damper my excitement over every other gift I opened after it that Christmas. I know I was only six or seven but it makes me sad to think about the disappointment my parents must've felt towards me that day. All I think of myself in that video is spoiled rotten.

We always had an abundance of gifts to walk into on Christmas mornings. I learned later in life that my mom stayed up into the wee hours of the morning every Christmas Eve setting up our living room so that everything would be perfect for us to come down to on Christmas morning. There was always a collection of gifts under the Christmas tree that were beautifully wrapped "From Mommy and Daddy". On the other side of the living room in a separately designated area, two pieces of furniture—one designated for me and one for Madeline—were covered in unwrapped gifts from Santa. It was every child's dream.

My mom always made things feel so special. Christmas, Valentine's Day, birthdays. She looked for any excuse to buy things for us. Gift giving was definitely her love language. She loved cards too. Every gift she gave included a card with a long handwritten, thoughtful note inside. I still have a lot of the cards she gave me over the years. For birthdays, Valentine's day, Christmas, just thinking of you, just missing you. The words in those cards mean so much more to me now than they did back then. Those words, in her handwriting, are some of my only remnants of her now. I read her words now and find it so easy to see how much she loved me, how thoughtful, sweet, and sincere she was. I meant so much to her.

1997 was a strange year for our little family. I was in second grade and seven years old. My sister in kindergarten, five years old. Some time that summer, she and I both came down with what my parents originally thought was a really bad stomach virus. I felt so bad that, to this day, I still vividly remember how miserable I felt as I clenched my stomach in excruciating pain from inside the bathroom stall at a Sounds' minor league baseball game. We used to go to their games on Friday nights and that's where we were when my symptoms first hit me. I'll never forget it. My parents said when we got home from that game, I climbed into our living room chair and slept for days. They had never seen me so lethargic. And just as I was finally starting to show signs of improvement, my sister came down with very similar symptoms. The difference between our experiences was that once she got sick, her health continued declining quickly and aggressively. When she showed signs of blood in her stool, my parents knew it had to be something more than a stomach bug.

Madeline was immediately taken to the hospital via ambulance from the pediatrician's office and admitted to Vanderbilt Children's Hospital for further evaluation soon thereafter. Within hours, she was diagnosed with E. coli O157 and remained there in that hospital for weeks. Through further testing, they found evidence of E. coli in my system as well. The doctors told my parents that for whatever reason, unlike my sister, my immune system somehow had strength to fight it off. The weeks Madeline was in the hospital were strange for me. I didn't understand the severity and complexity of the situation but knew it was serious because of the disruption it caused in our lives.

The state of Tennessee sits within what's known as "Dixie Alley," a region much like Tornado Alley, where severe weather—especially tornadoes—is a frequent and frightening reality. The area we lived in was no exception. I'll never forget the night my sister was admitted to the hospital—while we were already dealing with that chaos, tornadoes were ripping through our town. Both of my parents were at the hospital with Madeline and I was home with our babysitter. As the tornado sirens started wailing throughout our town and the power cut out, panic took over the house. I remember the babysitter's hands shaking as she cried and rushed to pull me into our "tornado closet"—the small, windowless space we had designated for emergencies like this. She was scared, clearly unsure of what to do, and I could feel that fear pulsing off of her. We huddled together for what felt like hours but was realistically probably only a few minutes.

Then, through the darkness and silence, I heard the front door open and my dad's voice calling my name. The moment I heard him, I broke down in tears. Relief hit me. I knew I was safe—because he was there.

Later, he told me he had literally seen that tornado trademark—the funnel of clouds—in his rear view mirror. He had to pull off the interstate multiple times because the winds were too strong to keep driving safely. But none of that stopped him. He pushed through the storm because he knew I was home and that I'd be afraid to be there without him or my mom. He knew I needed him just as much as Madeline did that night. He truly was always exactly where we needed him most.

Each set of grandparents took turns flying up to Tennessee to take care of me while both my parents were in the hospital with my sister for the weeks that followed. It was a really confusing time in my life. A few other kids from our school, who were also in the same after-school program with me and my sister, were also extremely sick with E. coli around that same time. This caused a big uproar with the media. In fact, I was asked to stay home from school for several days in the midst of it all because the local news stations had become an alarming and distracting presence at our elementary school.

The community rallied around us in ways I'll never forget.

Multiple blood drives were organized for my sister and the other sick students. My dad's coworkers generously donated their own PTO so he could remain by my sister's side without worrying about missing work. Our church family stepped up, bringing us meals, praying over my sister in her hospital room, and offering their help in any way they could.

We were surrounded by kindness, support, and more attention than we could have ever asked for—but even with all of that, all I really wanted was to have my mom and dad home again. To have our life feel normal again, even just for a moment.

My sister's health continued to decline before it finally began to improve. At her worst, she was diagnosed with kidney failure. I was told much later in life that at the worst of her health scare, they didn't know if she was going to make it.

"There's nothing left for us to do. There's nothing else we *can* do. She's in God's hands now."

That's what my parents were told.

But she didn't give up, she pulled through. She had a record of teetering on death's doorstep and beating the odds. Madeline was their delicate little flower. She always was and she always would be. This health scare made them cherish her even more than they did before.

Slowly but surely our life went back to normal. Madeline was eventually discharged and was gradually introduced back into the routine of everyday life. She spent that following summer in school—"summer school"—making up for the time she missed from class while she was so sick. Those few months were a time in my life I'll never forget. I think I was too young to really understand the extent of the situation. How serious it was and how traumatizing it would be for my parents—

watching their baby fight for her life. Meanwhile, I remember her coming home with a lot of new toys and I was jealous of her for that. Children are so naive.

In early 1999, my parents made the decision to move back to South Carolina and closer to family. Madeline's health scare made them realize how important it is to have family nearby—opposed to several states away like the situation we had gotten ourselves into when we made the move to Tennessee. We had an unmatched network of friends and a community we were forever indebted to for the support they provided us when we needed it most. But nothing compares to the love and support you have when family is right up the road. It's a safety net you can't match. Especially while raising young kids and attempting to maintain prospering careers of your own.

This job of my dad's—the one he had at this point in our lives—was actually the one he was able to carry with him back to South Carolina. He worked from home from that point on. My mom had no problem finding a new job herself. So the decision was made—1999 was the year we found ourselves back in South Carolina. We were exactly one town over and a short 30 minute drive from Williston—as new residents of Aiken, South Carolina. A place widely known as *Horse Country*.

15

the york street house

1999-2002

When we moved to Aiken, we bought another brick house situated right on the very desirable and conveniently located York Street SE. York Street runs through downtown Aiken and the SE portion of the street is lined with a collection of beautiful and eclectic homes full of southern charm.

Our house, specifically, was built in the 1950s and last updated in the 1970s before it became ours in 1999. The first thing my sister and I did when our family walked in with the real estate agent to see the house for the first time was lay down and make "snow angels" on the bright green (disgustingly old and dirty) shag carpet. My parents were mortified. I am too, 26 years later. We had never seen shag carpet before. Clearly we couldn't contain our excitement. My dad will never let us live that down.

This house was the definition of potential. It was a beautiful home with decadent features. We would be the house's third set of owners since it was built.

The original owners left residual evidence of what appeared to be a bit of paranoia while living there. Apparently when the first owner died, his widowed wife was extremely unsettled living in that house alone. She had keyed locks installed on every single window so that you could only open a window from the inside and with a key. But that in itself wasn't enough. Each window was also screwed shut. A bit strange. A key wouldn't do you any good if you didn't also have a screwdriver or a drill to remove the screws. There were a few other unusual remnants of her insecurities that I won't get into. It's just worth pointing out because it left a bit of an eerie energy in our new home.

The second set of owners were who we bought the house from. The man was an Italian Count and they only used the house as a winter vacation home. With the house, he left us two barely used cars and a 6-foot statue of a Knight's Guard in Medieval Armour. It was all a bit unusual. But that didn't stop my dad's excitement over their new white Mustang convertible and bright red Dodge Raider. My mom didn't let him keep the convertible for long, after hearing about a bad accident involving kids in the backseat of one.

My sister and I both had bedrooms upstairs in the York Street house. We'd both come downstairs in the mornings fairly regularly and tell our parents we heard footsteps the night before. They'd always quickly reassure us that we were just hearing squirrels on the roof. We'd argue with them that the squirrels sounded a lot like footsteps. They were insistent though.

When we were much older and more capable of handling the unsettling news, my dad told us he never believed in ghosts until we lived in that house. He said that on several occasions, when he was at home alone while we were at school and my mom was at work, he'd hear footsteps clear as day coming from upstairs. He told us that one time it was so convincing, he grabbed a gun and our dog (a little miniature schnauzer named Max) and quietly tiptoed up the two flights of stairs separating him from the potential intruder in our bedrooms. There was nothing. He said those footsteps he heard were so heavy, so obvious to be feet hitting the floor that he no longer believed the lie they were telling us about squirrels on the roof. He truly believed that house was haunted.

My dad worked tirelessly to perfect each and every room in this house. Maybe the ghosts were the real reason he worked so diligently, come to think of it. There was deep crown molding, a slate floored foyer and refinished hardwoods throughout the up and downstairs. I think his work here was what made the smell of polyurethane nostalgic for me. We, in essence, lived in a construction zone for most of our time here. It ended up being worth it though. The house was beautiful. Its current appraisal is over $600k more than what we paid for it back in 1999—if that says anything about the work he put into it.

These were the years my parents were both thriving in their careers. They were at a collective peak of success and my sister and I reaped the benefits of it. I danced for Aiken Ballet Company and spent most of my free time in ballet classes or at dance competitions. Madeline and I both also took horseback riding lessons and rode competitively at Fulmer International School of Equestrian. My dressage of first place ribbons from horse shows implied I was decently good at the sport. Unfortunately, I got bucked off of one of my favorite horses in a riding lesson one day, cracked my helmet, and never sat on a horse's back again.

Aiken was a beautiful place to live. Several of my mom's best girlfriends from high school lived there as well with their own families so we were able to spend a lot of time with them while we lived there. That York Street house was the last house I remember having a completely normal life in.

My dad told me while I was writing this book about a specific incident that happened late one night while living there. We had a home security system with an alarm my parents would activate every evening before they went to bed. My mom was more of a night owl than my dad so it wasn't unusual for her to stay up for several hours after he had called it a night. She'd stay out in the living room and watch TV, page through Southern Living magazines for project inspiration, hang out with the dogs. Just normal night owl things. Sometimes she'd even fall asleep on the couch before waking up in the wee hours of the morning to find her way back to their bedroom.

On this particular night, the night of the incident I'm referring to, it was after midnight when the doorbell rang. Given the time and the peculiarities of the situation, my dad jolted out of bed himself. Within just a few seconds of the doorbell ring, the security alarm started going off. If you aren't familiar with how these things work, this means an exterior door was opened to trigger the alarm. When this happens, you must act quickly to enter in your secret passcode to verify your safety. Otherwise, it's assumed you're in danger.

With this and obvious concern over the sound of a midnight alarm in mind, my dad jumped out of bed and quickly made his way out of their bedroom. Since a passcode hadn't been entered into the system timely enough, an agent from the security system company was already on the intercom installed in our house requesting our family passphrase. This was standard procedure for them before physically sending police to the location. If you couldn't make it to the alarm keypad to type in your passcode within the short, allotted amount of time, your only other chance to avoid a police visit was to share your passphrase verbally with the agent over the intercom.

With his own eyes on the situation, he quickly provided our passphrase to the agent to confirm our safety and continued making his way to the front of the house where he could see my mom standing with the front door wide open—talking to what appeared to be a homeless woman standing in front of her in our doorway. She then proceeded to leave the woman standing there alone and unaccompanied while she walked into the kitchen, grabbed cash from her purse, and made her way back to where my dad was now standing with the stranger. She reached around my dad, handed the unfamiliar woman the money, and told her to have a good night.

He couldn't believe how ignorant she was for opening the door for a stranger in the middle of the night. Even worse, leaving her there in our open doorway with free access to our home and family.

"What in hell were you thinking, Kellie?" My dad asked her, with fury in his tone.

"It was a homeless woman. She was just asking for money, Mark. Good grief. She needed help. She had no one to go to. " She mumbled irritably. As if he was the delusional one.

He could hear that her response was slurred and could see that her body language implied she wasn't totally coherent. And then she casually walked back into the living room and sat back under her blanket on the couch as if nothing happened.

In that moment, he knew something was deeply wrong. Her behavior was alarming—so far removed from the woman he had known and loved. She had always been the kind of person who would give the shirt off her back to a complete stranger without hesitation. But no matter how selfless she was, one line she had never crossed was putting her children in harm's way. That night, however, was different. Something had shifted. That night lingered with him for many years. It would mark the first time he saw that other side of her—the side of her he'd get to know very well in the years that followed.

Madeline and I slept through the events of that night. We had no idea what happened and we'd stay oblivious to it. It was a singular event and that's why it alarmed my dad as much as it did. It was unlike her. It was confusing and alarming.

The york street house was the last house we lived in where life felt totally normal for me. We lived in Aiken for almost three years and by the time we left York Street in 2002— relocating to Columbia for a job of my mom's—that house we left behind was absolutely astonishing. Ghosts and all. We kept that tidbit of information to ourselves when the house was listed. I'm sure the next buyers had their own stories to tell before long.

My mom and dad their senior year of high school (top left). Papaw John and my mom (bottom left). Barbara and my mom (bottom right).

Local newspaper clipping of my parents' engagement announcement (left). My mom's bridal portrait (right).

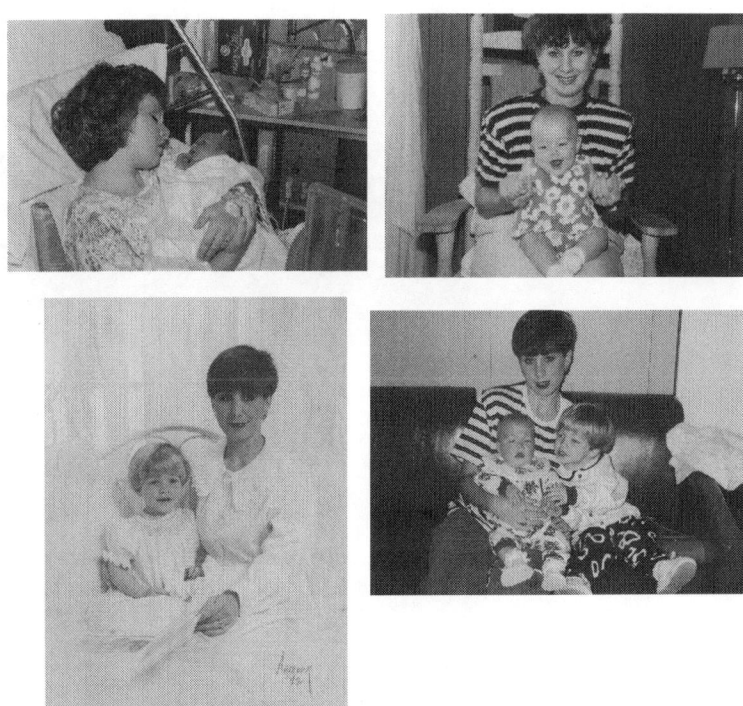

My mom holding me the day I was born, March 14, 1990 (top left). Me and my mom (top right). Me and my mom with our matching bowl cuts (bottom left). My mom, sister, and me (bottom right).

THE HOUSE THAT BROKE ME

THE YORK STREET HOUSE

III

Part Three

January 7, 2015 and the days that followed

16

a normal wednesday

january 7, 2015

I've convinced myself that I've forgotten a lot of over the years due to having three children in a short two year span of time. I'm not sure if having kids and the exhaustion that comes with it really causes memory loss but I feel like the older I get, the less I remember about the little details of passing moments. My best friends will bring up stories from 10-15 years ago and talk about it in such detail it was as if it happened yesterday. Stories I have absolutely no recollection of—such little remembrance. It's almost as if I wasn't actually there. Though they swear I was.

Maybe it's the years of deprived sleep that comes with having young kids or maybe it's just my version of getting older–the beginning of memory loss. Or maybe, just maybe, it's grief to blame. Maybe it really is the grief I've experienced that has replaced those seemingly insignificant, simple moments in time with the vivid details of what unexpectedly and tragically became the worst night of my entire life. The latter would make sense. Grief certainly seems to overtake the space it's given. It simply becomes a part of you. It defines you, consumes you. Once faced with loss in its most devastating form, you aren't the same person. How can you be? The truth is, you'll never again be who you were before you were dealt the hand of grief. Or at least that's what it's done to me. That's been my entire experience in a nutshell over these past 10 years.

I'll never forget the night of January 7, 2015. I can't remember what I had for dinner two nights ago or what I wore to work yesterday but I remember exactly where I was standing, what I was thinking, how I was feeling in the moments leading up to receiving the most devastating news of my life that night an entire decade ago. It was such a normal night. It was such a normal Wednesday until it became a Wednesday I'd never forget.

I was living the stereotypical life of an unmarried, young professional in January of 2015. I worked fairly long days throughout the week and enjoyed social outings on the weekends with new and old friends. I'd been working with the company I still work for today for a little over a year by this point, in early 2015. This job of mine was and still is in IT. It still blows my mind to say out loud—that I work in IT. Apparently IT is a fitting field for people with math degrees like me. I had no plan for the future or reason for pursuing that path— studying math—other than just loving the subject. I loved the challenge of having to think through a problem to find the answer. Granted, the level of math I studied in college ended up being more Greek characters than actual numbers. When it got to that point, I started to lose focus of what I was even trying to accomplish anymore. But I still loved it. I've always loved a challenge. You get every bit of a good challenge when you work through your first 10 page mathematical proof. I did lots of those in my time at Clemson. But that's beside the point. IT is just not where I would've ever imagined myself being one day. But here I am. And honestly, I kind of get it. I get why it works. Math people like to problem solve and a big part of working in IT *is* problem solving. The two go hand-in-hand. Like two peas in a pod.

Within the first year of my career in IT, I had surprisingly formed pretty close friendships with several of my coworkers. I found the nerdy IT guys to be my preferred peers—no time or care for drama, desert dry sense of humor, entirely different interests from my own. I enjoyed their friendships. Mostly because they were easy company but they were also just genuinely good people. I'm sure I brought more emotion and sensitivity to our work space than they preferred at times but they never made me feel unwanted. In fact, I always felt welcome, respected, even "at home" when I was with them.

Back then I didn't realize how much of life is spent with coworkers. How much you grow to know and care about these people. How many significant life events, milestones you experience over time with your coworkers often being one of the few constants by your side through all of them. Dating, marriage, divorce, pregnancy, births, deaths, promotions, demotions, everything. They're by your side through it all. It may be involuntary, but they're still *there.* Even if it's just in a literal sense. Those familiar faces working from cubicles alongside you become that sacred sense of normalcy you yearn for and learn to cherish when times are tough.

I obviously didn't have this wise and sentimental perspective on my coworkers back in 2015. But I do now. It took me time and significant loss to realize how much they meant to me even back then. Even if I didn't look at them with such deep perspective 10 years ago, I did recognize them as people I enjoyed being around and cared about. The faces I looked forward to seeing on Monday mornings after just having counted down the minutes to the 5:00 p.m. farewell the Friday prior. They had quickly become some of my best friends.

The month prior, which would've been mid-December 2014, I had just started dating a new guy. He was good friends with my best friend Tracy's boyfriend. They introduced the two of us at Christmas party. This guy came along at just the right time to get me over the incredibly hard breakup I went through a few months prior with the guy, Dan, from New York. Things had taken a positive turn and were going surprisingly well in my life—just in time for ringing in the new year of 2015. 2014 had been a challenging year for me with loss and heartbreak in several forms. But 2015 was a new start. I was 24, had a successful career, a new guy I was pretty smitten over, a solid group of close friends. I had found my groove again.

On the evening of January 7, 2015, Tracy and I went out for sushi with a group of coworkers. We were celebrating a friend's birthday a week late because he was born on Christmas Eve. Poor James. He always hated the fact that his birthday was on Christmas Eve because it was naturally and understandably easily overshadowed by arguably the most important day of the year. Christmas. And yes, the reference to "coworkers" included Tracy. We were (and still are) also coworkers. Not only did I get to hang out with my best friend on the weekends but we ended up working for the same company after college as well. Both of us in IT. So we weren't just working for the same company—we were in the same division of the organization, the same department, even had the same boss. I say this like it's some huge and ironic coincidence but there really aren't that many big employers in our area. It was kind of funny that we ended up working for the same boss though.

Funny enough, when we first started working together, our cubes were right beside each other. We had half wall cubes so we might as well have shared a space. Two chairs pulled up to the same desk. That would've been a sight to see. We literally couldn't have been placed any closer. It didn't take long before it was fairly obvious productivity would increase with a different seating arrangement. Not that we weren't professional, but we were long time best friends and everyone knew it.

17

tracy

It's astonishing the number of people who have asked me and Tracy if we are sisters over the years. It could be that we work for the same (IT) company and are the same age, height, brown hair color, similar-ish builds. I guess this means, by default, we look the same. In a field with a high population of older men, young females do tend to stand out. If you get close enough, you'll see that we look nothing alike. But I can kind of see it from far away. Especially if all you can see is the back of our brown-haired heads.

Tracy's dad—who I call "Uncle Steve"—is 50% Japanese (his mom was from Japan) which makes Tracy a quarter Japanese. She's always been told that she's got an exotic beauty about her and I'd have to agree. I've always appreciated the rare and natural beauty she possesses—those little details that make her unmistakably herself. She's a natural beauty and doesn't need to wear makeup to look put together like some of us. She's got olive skin, a toned physique, dark brown hair, radiant hazel eyes. And then there's me—fair skin, naturally dark blonde hair, bright blue eyes. When you break down our features like this, our appearances sound like polar opposites. That's why it's comical for us to be asked if we're sisters.

I love Tracy's parents. To know them is to love them. Once you get to know Steve and Debby, it's easy to see how Tracy turned out to be the human she is. I have a very vivid memory of a time with her dad. I think it was in that moment I recognized the pureness in his soul. A group of our friends from college had stayed at Tracy's parents' house—the house she grew up in—the prior night before heading downtown Columbia to tailgate for the USC/Clemson game that Saturday morning. I believe it was 2011, our senior year of college. This was another one of those periods of time when I was struggling with random, severe bouts of nausea for unexplained reasons. The joys of IBS. We all woke up that morning excited for the football game. Out of nowhere, I started feeling extremely sick to my stomach. I had gotten a text from my dad earlier that morning insinuating that my mom was having another series of really bad days and he was upset over it himself. Looking back, it's easy to see the correlation between that and the physical symptoms I was experiencing that morning but it didn't seem so obvious then.

While everyone was getting hyped up and loading tailgate essentials into their cars to caravan downtown, I stood back in the kitchen with hesitation and embarrassment. I knew I'd look lame and pathetic for telling everyone I wasn't going to be able to make it—that I wasn't feeling well and was going to drive to my parents house instead. I was carrying so much weight on my heart and in my mind over the situation back at home. A situation most were completely oblivious to. Instead,

I just looked lame for bowing out of drinking plans last minute. The lame friend who decides to miss out on the biggest football game of the year because her tummy hurts.

All of these feelings compounded at the same time Steve walked over to me in the kitchen and said, "K-wood—you okay? You better go out there. I don't want them to leave without you."

He called me K-wood because for the longest time, I thought I wanted to go to law school and be a lawyer like my dad. I also had blonde hair back then. I reminded him of Elle Woods from Legally Blonde. Elle Woods turned into K-wood and that was my nickname that stuck.

In that moment, standing there in their kitchen, he was the only person I had to fall apart to. And that's exactly what I did. I didn't say a word. I just walked over, collapsed into his arms, and cried. I don't remember exactly what I said but I know I told him I wasn't feeling well and really just wanted to go home. I remember he comforted me and reassured me that no one was going to give me a hard time for taking care of myself. He walked outside and told them I wasn't coming. I stood there in the kitchen until everyone left and then drove back to my parents house in Williston. I don't know if Steve knew there was more to it than it seemed on the surface. I'm guessing he probably did—parents aren't dumb. What I do know is that he was there when I needed him. I'll never forget that interaction of ours. He may not have thought anything of it—not a single second thought. But it's stayed with me for many years. I love him for it.

Tracy and I went to the same middle school and the same high school. Both of us proud Blythewood Middle School and Blythewood High School alumni. For whatever reason, we always found ourselves in different circles with strikingly different friend groups all throughout middle and high school. Tracy's clique was the type your parents hoped you'd find yourself a part of. The kind you'd gladly, with no ounce of hesitation, bring home to meet your parents. They were just genuinely good people. Church goers, community service volunteers, academically driven and inclined individuals. They were the kids that filled up the AP class rosters and made acing all of the tests I found extremely difficult to pass look easy. They spent most of their Saturday nights together in one of their family's living rooms watching movies or college football—depending on the season. They had a safe and respected idea of fun. I admired and respected each of them. Including Tracy.

My high school friends, on the other hand, were your stereotypical party crowd. I met most of my close girl friends when I started cheering in high school. Even the varsity cheerleading squad was divided between the good girls and the party girls. I was one of the party girls. Like myself, most of my friends were dating guys on the varsity lacrosse team so our friend group was comprised mostly of cheerleaders and lacrosse players. Funny that it played out like that because you always hear about cheerleaders dating football players. The lacrosse guys were way more fun at our high school. And our idea of fun was often unsafe and not responsible. We had a great time but we also tended to attract trouble. Really, we were just dumb kids who found creative ways to gain access to alcohol and fake IDs by 16. We threw parties in open fields and those parties were almost always ended abruptly by local law enforcement. On the nights we didn't get caught, we'd strategically stay out until 5:00 a.m. just so we could be around when McDonald's switched back over to their breakfast menu. We'd order bacon, egg, and cheese biscuits, eat them from our car in the parking lot, and then sneak back into whosoever house we were staying at before the sun came up.

The scariest run in we had with law enforcement happened at a party on winter break when I came back home to visit after my first semester at Clemson. I went with my friends to a party in an area of town that I don't think any of us were overly familiar with at the time. I'm honestly not sure how we ended up there or how we even heard about it. About an hour into the party, we heard a fight break out in the front yard. Fights always happened at parties we went to and I never understood why. Apparently people just liked to get drunk and fight each other. It was so dumb.

But this fight was no ordinary fight. I realized that when people started yelling, "they have guns!!!"

Oh shit. This was definitely not a normal party fight.

I had ridden with my boyfriend and one of his friends to that party in his parents' minivan which meant I didn't have my own easy method for escape. But you didn't have to say the word "guns" twice to kick my butt into gear. I was resourceful when I needed to be.

I guess my form of survival instinct kicked in because I somehow managed to quickly find the guy I rode with in the sea of panicked drunk people. I grabbed his keys straight from his front pocket and took off running to the van. I didn't check to see who was following me or offer others an invitation to safety. I just took control of the situation and acted fast. Regardless of why it played out the way it did, it made the most sense for me to be the one driving us away from the party anyway. I was probably the most sober of all of us. I was pretty good at reading the room—using context clues to help me decide how comfortable I was in a situation. From the moment we walked in, I knew that party was not a comfortable situation for me.

I jumped in that mini van as fast as I could and yelled to my friends, "I'm leaving, NOW. Either get in or you're stuck here."

If my memory serves me correctly, I was halfway down the road before their bodies were fully enclosed in the vehicle and the sliding doors were completely clasped shut. It couldn't have even been 20 seconds of leaving the driveway before I saw blue lights in the rear view mirror.

"Whoever is driving the vehicle, pull the car over now. I repeat, whoever is driving the vehicle, pull over immediately." They instructed me over their intercom system.

My right leg was shaking uncontrollably. I could barely operate the vehicle at that point because of how nervous I was. For some reason, I kept driving. I think I was too focused on getting away from the house with the guns—the whole reason I was involuntarily driving the van in the first place—that I physically couldn't allow myself to pull over. I just kept chugging along, at a snail's pace of 5 mph, my foot bouncing up and down against the gas peddle like I was a crack addict. I wished I had an intercom system on that minivan so I could reassure those cops I wasn't fleeing the scene. Just a little 19 year old girl completely freaking out without a clue as to what to do with a parade of cop cars following her.

As soon as I got us back onto one of the main streets and out of the sketchy neighborhood we'd somehow found ourselves in, I pulled into the first store parking lot I could see. A rim shop—like one of those used rim shops that have names like "RIM-Z" graffiti'd on the side of the building. Yeah, one of those. If that helps you understand the area of town we were in.

By the time I finally pulled the van over, the three or four cop cars that had collected behind us quickly formed a barricade around us. You know, in case we tried to flee the scene. If only they knew the type of kids they were dealing with. We weren't going anywhere. Still speaking over their intercom system, they instructed us to exit the vehicle with our hands in the air. We followed their orders and lined up, hands in the air, facing the secondhand rim store. I was bawling the entire time. It was one thing to be at a party and have the cops shut it down. But this time, I had three cop cars ordering me to pull a van over that wasn't my own as I was fleeing the scene of a shooting.

The cops spoke with each of us. I was first because I was the one driving the van. While sobbing uncontrollably, I explained the situation and begged him not to arrest me. I told him my parents would kill me if I lost my college scholarships. I don't remember him having much pity for me though. They called my house and my dad eventually showed up to pick me up shortly after 2:00 a.m.

"Did you perform a breathalyzer on her?" My dad asked the officer.

The officer whispered to my dad, "No and I can tell you that your daughter didn't do anything wrong here. We only handled things the way we did to frighten them. They should've never been over here. This is a dangerous area. Maybe they'll think twice next time they consider going to a party in an unfamiliar area."

As I was getting in my dad's car, the officer yelled, "You Blythewood bumpkins need to stick to your field parties. You have no business being over here."

"Clearly." I thought to myself.

TRACY

My dad didn't speak a word to me the whole 30 minute drive home. I cried and apologized over and over but he never said a word in response. This was the worst kind of punishment from him. Silence. Disappointment. Shame.

"Get out of the car and go take a shower. You smell like beer and cigarettes." He said as he slammed the car door behind him, walked inside, and left me by myself in the parking lot of the apartment complex they were living in.

I passed my mom on the couch as I was walking inside. She was glaring at me with equal disappointment.

"I can't believe you'd do something like this. What were you THINKING?" I could hear disgust in her tone.

I didn't answer her. I rolled my eyes and kept walking. She was one to talk.

I'll never forget how safe I felt in the apartment that night. How I'd never take being free and not in the custody of law enforcement for granted ever again. I told myself that night as I was trying to force myself to fall asleep, tossing and turning, that I'd never come back to see my high school friends again. I didn't mean it, of course. But I was angry with myself that I had even gotten into that kind of situation. I had worked so hard to get into Clemson and I almost threw it all away. At least that's what I thought. I learned a hard lesson that night.

As you can see, we were trouble but I loved my friends. To this day, I think back on those wild years as some of the best of my life. With the exception of the rim shop night, most of the fun we had was dumb but innocent teenage fun. Those fun nights were an escape from the reality of my life at home that was quickly unraveling.

Tracy and I really connected for the first time during our senior year AP Calculus class. One thing to mention is that while I did enjoy Saturday night beer pong and flip cup, I also worked really hard in school and I loved math. That's how I found myself as a close acquaintance of the good kids in school, like Tracy. We shared a lot of the same AP (Advanced Placement) classes, Calculus being one of them.

We still joke that we met by both being part of the dumb half of the Calculus class. Apparently at some point midway through the school year, they split our class up into AB and BC. BC being a more advanced and comprehensive version of AB calculus. There is formality to it - AB and BC - but to us, it meant dumb and smart. It didn't take a rocket scientist to figure out that someone, somewhere labeled a few of us as not smart enough for BC. The dumb kids. So the AB students sat on the right side of the room and the BC students on the left. While the BC students continued progressing through their advanced and more prestigious calculus material, the AB students—myself included—got to slow down a bit and relearn what we'd already been taught. It worked itself out eventually I guess. I did, in fact, end up with a Mathematics degree. It really is all relative I guess. Being in AP Calculus at all meant something to be proud of in high school.

AB wasn't so bad after all. I like to think our side of the classroom had more fun. We could take our time and relax a little bit. That's also where I met and got to know Tracy. So I guess I owe Coach Curry (our AP calc teacher) a special thanks for putting us together in the dumb half of the class. That decision of his changed my life.

The second half of senior year was when most of us pretty much knew what our plans would be for after graduation. Like I said before, I applied to four South Carolina schools, got accepted by all of them, and ultimately went with my first choice: Clemson University. It came up in conversation one day on the dumb side of AP Calculus that Tracy had also decided on Clemson. Ironically, neither of us had plans for a roommate.

One of the guys in our class named Tanner, who we'd become good friends with at Clemson, jokingly said one day, "So Kate, you're going to Clemson and Tracy, you're going to Clemson. Yall should be roomies."

That was it. That's all it took. The rest was history. Tanner loves to take credit for matchmaking us.

Tracy and I lived together all four years of college which I think surprised us both. We were only acquaintances in high school and we both knew there was a reason for that—we had different interests, different definitions of "fun", we were just *different* in many ways.

Our freshman year, we shared a cinder block dorm room in a building called the *Shoeboxes* which pretty much lived up to its name. The same dorm room my bottle of pain medication went missing from after my dental emergency. It was a tiny little 11'x16' space for the two of us to eat, sleep, study, hang out, watch tv. All the same activities I now require a 3600 sqft house to do. It's no wonder we became so close.

Some time our freshman year, my mom accepted a job in Greenville, South Carolina which was only about 45 minutes away from us in Clemson. This was one of those jobs she'd start off loving and seemingly thriving in until she got too comfortable, brought her addiction with her to work, and inevitably had to say goodbye. Before things went downhill with her job in Greenville, Tracy and I were actually able to spend some time with her being right up the road from us. We really looked forward to our time with her actually. She'd come pick us up from our dorm room in the evening when she got off work, either take us out to dinner or have dinner delivered to her Greenville apartment, and we'd have a sleepover there with her. We'd watch movies or just stay up talking and laughing. Just like every other living space she touched, her little apartment was the perfect balance of beauty and comfort. She always had a bed setup for each of us in the living area—sheets, blankets, quilts, pillows, everything—before we'd even arrived. She'd have fresh towels and washcloths waiting by the clean shower—a luxury we had grown unaccustomed to from months of sharing dorm showers with 40 other girls on our floor. She wanted us to feel at home as soon as we walked in. She took good care of us while we were with her. All three of us were sad for her to drop us back off that next morning. Watching her drive away made me homesick every time. I feel confident Tracy still carries these memories of our time with my mom in Greenville as well. Those nights spent the three of us introduced Tracy to the mom I had on good days—the mom I used to have every day, when every day with her was a good day and our lives were much happier.

We moved into another on-campus apartment our sophomore year at Clemson. Calhoun Courts is what that living space was called. Unit S9B. Tracy and I shared a room and a bunk bed again in this apartment. But now that we were in an actual apartment instead of just a little dorm room, we had to be matched with two other girls who lived in the other room of the apartment. The two other girls didn't know each other beforehand and I don't think either of them spoke to one another the entire year we lived in that unit. They were both extremely quiet and had no interest in being friendly with me or Tracy. In fact, if they heard us coming into the apartment, they'd quickly flee the living and kitchen area and sneak back into their bedroom. We were pretty sure one of the girls had bulimia based on the sounds we'd hear coming from our shared bathroom. The other girl was always studying or cooking extravagant dishes. We'd come home after a late night of drinking and eat her beautifully dished lasagnas straight out of their casserole dishes. I feel kind of guilty about it nowadays. I'm sure Tracy does too. We just thought they were strange and unfriendly and therefore had no shame in our actions as a result of our feelings on them.

Our sophomore year of college was when we really got into the party scene. Not that I wasn't already familiar with the party scene from high school but I like to think getting closer to Tracy our freshman year helped calm me down a little. We went to frat parties and dressed up in trash bags (don't ask) to go along with what it seemed like everyone else was doing. But aside from that, we were relatively calm our freshman year. We were also engineering majors that first year. Engineering at Clemson is not for the faint of heart. That's all I have to say about that. It wasn't for me—I took it as a sign that was the case by my dad having to help me with every hands-on assignment that year.

I'll never forget the last project we were tasked with to wrap up our General Engineering class. We had to create a device that only required a single action to initiate it's movement. The device had to be able to smoothly make it's way up and down a predefined ramp and then come to a controlled stop. It couldn't have a motor or remote control of any kind. Ha. Tracy's older brother was a senior that year. A Mechanical Engineering major—one of the big guys. I was so proud to bring my little man made vehicle to show off to him. I set that contraption down on the ground to show off my hard work, removed the rubber band to initiate its departure, and all four wheels immediately flew off. This clearly did not go as I planned. Her brother and his friend laughed, I cried, and that's when I decided engineering was not for me.

Tracy and I both decided to try out sorority rush week our sophomore year. I don't know why we did it—Greek life wasn't really fitting for either of us. Neither of us got any of the sororities we wanted and both eventually dropped out of the sorority we pledged. There was one positive of the experience though. Going through rush week is where we met our best friend Sammi.

Sammi was unlike any girl we'd ever met in our little confined world of South Carolina. From Freehold, New Jersey she was the definition of a force to be reckoned with. Everything about Sammi was totally new to us. Her style, her personality, her accent—a thick Jersey accent. But aside from the accent, nothing about her was what I had always imagined a Jersey girl to be. Granted, all I knew of New Jersey was what I saw on Jersey Shore.

She has fair skin like me and a very trendy sense of style. She didn't wear white skirts and polo shirts with jack roger sandals like every girl from South Carolina wore in 2009. She wore dresses that complimented her curvy figure and danced to the beat of her own drum. She was and still is the biggest feminist I've ever known. She has strong political views but isn't just talk, she actually knows what she's talking about and has educated reasons for the grounds she stands on.

I feel like Sammi has always been the most responsible of our friend group. She was the friend you'd be mad at for telling you you'd had enough to drink and insisting that she get you home. But she was also the friend you'd thank the next morning for taking care of you and watching out for you. She's always been the most independent, the most decisive, the most headstrong. I think Tracy and I have both learned a lot from our friendship with Sammi. She's made us both better women and better humans.

Tracy, Sammi, and I lived together in a townhouse in Pendleton, South Carolina our junior and senior years of college. Sammi continued being the responsible friend—she kept our house beautifully decorated and as clean and clutter-free as possible in a college town. Our townhouse was nice and large so it naturally became a good space for parties. We had quite a few 21st birthdays in that Pendleton townhouse. Mine was Justin Bieber themed—the biggest love of my life at 21. My friends hung a life sized Justin Bieber printout on my bedroom door for that party. They knew the way to my heart.

Over the four years we spent at Clemson together, Tracy and I evolved from two acquaintances sharing a bunk bed and an alarm clock to genuinely best friends.

We barely ever fought and I'm still not quite sure why. I say barely ever but I genuinely can't remember a single fight we had all four of those years. Knowing both of us now, I'm not sure how we put up with each other as effortlessly as we did for such a long period of time. Living in such close quarters. We each have our own version of strong mindedness. Tracy is competitive and I'm a perfectionist. We both get worked up and frustrated over the same things but we both handle those emotions completely differently. I guess our similarities and differences were perfectly balanced. We had just the right amount of commonalities and distinctions to create a friendship capable of withstanding the tests of time.

We spent most of our time together in college laughing. I

have to share one of my favorite Tracy and Kate stories. Sammi jokes that this story defines our friendship and who we are when we're together.

Tracy and I were the definition of fad dieters. We did it all—cabbage soup, baby food, tomato soup, liquid. You name it, we've tried it. One night on our way back to our townhouse in Pendleton from the library, we decided to stop at Wendy's and get junior bacon cheeseburgers and fries (a Kate and Tracy crowd favorite). We were both starving but didn't want Sammi and our other roommate, Mia, to judge us for not staying loyal to the diet the four of us were doing together. Our only option was to scarf down our food quickly while we were driving home so that by the time we got home, we could pretend like we were staying dedicated by going to sleep with growling stomachs.

As we shoved food in our mouths while I drove my Nissan Sentra down that dark highway, Tracy began laughing so hard no sound was even coming out of her mouth. Without even knowing what she was losing herself over, I immediately found myself joining in with her laughter. We had that effect on each other—when one of us laughed, the other had to join in. I remember laughing so hard, I could barely drive down the road. I'm surprised we didn't get pulled over. As soon as she had a moment to regain her composure, she explained to me that she was shoveling fries in her mouth so fast that she unknowingly devoured a salt packet along with them. She thought the fries tasted extra salty until she realized she was chewing on a piece of paper. When she pulled the paper out of her mouth, she saw remnants of the soggy "SALT" label. This only made us both laugh harder. To this day, I don't think I've ever laughed so hard in my life. We simply refer to this night as "Salt Packet" now.

TRACY

The majority of my best memories in college were because Tracy was a part of them. I'd love to go back and relive some of those days together. We get very little time together nowadays, now that we're both married with children of our own. But she's still the only person that consistently makes me laugh until my belly hurts.

My mom told me early on my freshman year of college that Tracy was going to be the friend I'd need in life. It's almost like she had a premonition. As soon as she had enough time around Tracy to get to know her and understand her, she became one of my mom's favorite humans. She would always tell me how lucky I was to have someone like her and that I should never take our friendship for granted.

"Friends like her don't just come along, Kate. You'll realize it one day." I remember rolling my eyes at her, thinking to myself, *you're just glad I'm not hanging out with my high school friends anymore.*

But parents are wise, they know what they're talking about. And my mom was right, friends like her don't just come along. She was also right about her being the friend I'd need in life. I would need Tracy more than any of us could've ever imagined. I'd need her more than most females in their early 20s could ever need their best friend.

18

a not so normal wednesday

january 7, 2015

Winters in South Carolina are unusual and predictably unpredictable. It could be 80 degrees on Christmas and snowing just a week later on New Year's Day. On this particular Wednesday evening, January 7, 2015, the weather was what you'd expect for early January. Chilly.

After wrapping up dinner and drinks at the sushi spot, we said our "goodbyes" and "see you at work tomorrows" and all went off to do whatever young professionals with no kids do on work nights. I couldn't wait to get back to my one bedroom apartment. To immediately take off my makeup, change into my pajamas, and cuddle up on the couch with my dogs. This particular apartment I was living in was once shared with my ex-boyfriend from New York and our two dogs, Rocky and Rucker. When he told me he was moving back to New York to be closer to his family, I told him he couldn't leave and also take the dogs—so the dogs became *my* dogs and they stayed with me.

It's so bizarre to think back to the days of being able to just mindlessly go to dinner with coworkers. To stay out as late as I wanted to and do whatever I wanted to because I had no real responsibilities waiting back at home for me. I wouldn't trade the beautiful life I have now for anything and I really mean that. I'm not just saying it because I feel obligated to in case my kids read this book one day. Bars and staying out past 8:00 p.m. don't sound the least bit appealing to me anymore. But that freedom and flexibility to think and act selflessly at all times is something you really can't appreciate until it becomes a distant memory. When you and your spouse decide that you might be ready to start a family—you really don't even know what ready that means. You don't have a clue, before you have children of your own, how much those children will change *everything*. That's why it feels crazy to even say that my entire night plans entailed dinner with coworkers and going straight home to change into my pajamas and sit on the couch with my dogs. It's like I've lived two entirely different lives in one.

The night of January 7, 2015, I pulled into my apartment around 8:00 pm. My dogs were super excited to see me, as they always were no matter how long I had been away. I once read that dogs have no concept of time. Ten minutes or ten hours, it's all the same to them. I don't know if that makes me feel better or worse. I always felt guilty leaving them for so long while I was at work. At least they had each other, I suppose. At least the two of them were benefiting from sharing a space with another puppy similar in age to their own. For some reason it seemed like a good idea at the time to get two very young puppies within a couple months of each other. I wanted Rocky to have a friend so three months after getting him (my Boston

Terrier), I got Rucker (my Boxer). Neither of my dogs were even a year old in early 2015. They were still full of youth and loads of energy. I lived on the second floor of my apartment building so going outside with two dogs was a task in and of itself. I was convinced I was the talk of the apartment community on multiple occasions after chasing them through the parking lot in my work heels when they'd get off their leashes during our after-work walk. A quick bathroom break turned into a game of cat and mouse more times than I could count. It was a sight to see, I'm sure of it. They were a handful. But I loved them and they never gave me a dull moment—or a break.

I took the dogs out for a quick (uneventful) walk as soon as I got home from dinner that night and stayed committed to my plans of immediate makeup removal and pajamas soon thereafter. It was just a normal Wednesday work night. The next day would be a normal Thursday with only one more work day to go before the weekend. I remember I was already exchanging texts with Tracy who had just gotten back to her house and was watching a movie with her boyfriend. What is it about best friends? It's like you can never talk to each other too much. You can never share too much. They know you better than you ever know yourself.

The guy I had just started seeing was still new to me so I overthought every message I sent to him. Once I settled on the right wording to use in my text to him, I pulled the trigger and hit send. All the overthinking and worry to simply ask him how his day was. I set my phone down on the bathroom sink and walked into my living area to turn on the TV when I heard the sound of a new text notification. I hoped it was a response from that guy but realistically that would've been too quick of a response. It's not like he was sitting around staring at his phone waiting for me to reach out to him. It was much more likely another text from Tracy. Either way, I'd look in a few minutes. My phone wasn't going anywhere. I had to play it cool just in case it was him anyway—I didn't want to seem overly eager. There was nothing attractive about a girl who responds back to a text within seconds of receipt. I wasn't going to be that girl. So I casually finished what I was doing in my room with a little pep in my step, of course. After picking out my outfit for work the next day, I walked back into the bathroom to grab my phone with anticipation.

I think most cell phones have this "lift to wake feature" that allows the phone to illuminate without actually having to be physically touched. Though its name implies you have to be physically holding it for it to light up, I'm pretty sure phones have a situational awareness—like they can sense you coming close and go ahead and light themselves up for convenience. At least that's how mine have always behaved.

On this particular evening, my phone could've spared me those couple seconds. I could've used just a few more moments of life as I knew it. Just a few more seconds of normalcy, at least what I knew as normalcy those days. But it was too late, before I was even given the opportunity to pick the phone up off the counter, the screen illuminated and I saw the unread message. It was the last person I ever would've imagined receiving a text from on a random Wednesday night. The text was from my then-brother-in-law.

Madeline and I are coming to pick you up. Something tragic has happened at your parent's house.

My heart sank.

19

the worst wednesday imaginable

I knew in my gut the moment I read that text that the tragedy was my mom. In the back of my mind, I always knew this day would come. How could it not? A psychiatrist my mom saw for several years once told my dad during a session that she was playing Russian roulette with her life every time she opened up those pill bottles. My dad telling me that really stuck with me. It scared me to death because I knew he was right. That psychiatrist was warning her that she was playing a dangerous game with her very own existence here on this earth. She was the only one with the power to choose not to pull the trigger.

Just like that doctor, I also knew that one day the odds just wouldn't be in her favor anymore. Odds could only be in her favor for so long while playing such a dangerous game like she was. I just didn't know when or where I'd be when it happened. Even if I did somehow know when it would happen and where I'd be, I could've never possibly prepared for it.

I didn't respond to my brother-in-law's text but instead

called my parents' house. He and I were not close and in all honesty, I didn't care much for him. I tried several times over the years and could just never find it in me to have pleasant feelings towards him. If something tragic happened that involved my own parents, he was not who I was going to hear it from.

Even though I knew in my heart what the tragedy was, part of me was holding onto hope that maybe something happened to one of their dogs. The unexpected loss of one of their dogs would be devastating, absolutely. They'd had those dogs forever. Or, a more likely theory, my dad might've finally decided he just couldn't take it any longer—the ups and mostly downs with my mom—and wanted a divorce. He had threatened it more times than I could count over the years. Every time the word came up, my sister and I would cry and beg for them not to. A life without them together just wasn't fathomable for us. Back then, it felt like the worst possible outcome for our little family of four. But if that were the case—if they *had* finally decided to move forward with a divorce—why wouldn't they just call me and tell me themselves? Why would I need to be picked up by my brother-in-law on a Wednesday night when I have work the next day. My parents knew that. Those wouldn't be reasons that justified the reality of what was unfolding.

He used the word "tragic" in his text. I noticed that immediately, as if it were in bold font in the message he sent. Tragic was such a heavy word. Also relative depending on opinion, perception, and personal experiences. I didn't view my brother-in-law as one to ever really exaggerate. He also didn't use dramatic words like "tragic" in routine conversation. Regardless, I needed to find out for myself what was going on at my parents house and I didn't want to hear it from anyone but them.

We still had a landline in 2015. We called it our *home phone.* This was the number we'd dial when we knew or at least expected someone to be home to answer. I still have that phone number memorized. Cell phones were used when everyone was assumed to be away from the house. But at 9:00 p.m. on a Wednesday night, both of my parents would certainly be home.

I dialed our home phone number first. No answer. I tried again. No answer. As my heart began racing, I moved on to their cell phones. I called my dad's first. No answer. Then my mom's. No answer.

As if the text of something tragic happening at home wasn't enough to tell me something was not right back at home, the reality of their not answering any of my calls filled me with immediate panic. With shaking hands, I took a deep breath and resumed my efforts to reach someone back at my parents' house. I called over and over until finally, someone picked up. I was met with silence on the other end of the line.

"Hello?"

[Silence]

".... Mommy?"

[Silence]

"....Daddy?..."

It was deafening silence until it wasn't. And that's when I heard my dad's blood curdling screams. I will never forget that silence followed by the chillingly desolate and agonizing devastation in his cries. The strongest man I'd ever known had finally broken.

I couldn't make out much of what he was saying but I heard enough for the strength in my legs to give out as I fell to my knees right there in my apartment bedroom. I remember exactly where I was standing. I was on the right side of the foot of my bed. Right there is where I curled up on the carpet, into the fetal position, and felt my heart break into two. My dad didn't need to say a thing. The second I heard him crying like that—loud, broken, guttural—I just knew. Only three people in this world could wreck him like that and I knew two of us were safe. The tragedy was my mom. She was gone. Just like that. And calling it a tragedy doesn't even come close. January 7, 2015, ripped my world apart. It was the worst day of my life.

The rest of the night was a vividly crisp blur. There was really no other way to describe it. None of it made sense. It was as if I was quickly removed from my own body with occasional glimpses, here and there, from behind my own eyes.

After I got off the phone with my dad, the first person I called was Tracy. I remember it sounded like I had woken her up or interrupted something. She didn't sound annoyed, she just sounded caught off guard which I'm sure I reciprocated in my own tone. I've never been much of a phone talker so a call from me in itself was strange. Much less a call from me at close to 10:00 p.m. on a Wednesday night.

"Hey, I'm sorry to bother you. I know it's late. You're never going to believe what happened...my mom died," the words escaped my mouth faster than I could think them.

I couldn't believe it.

It was the first time I said it out loud. It was long before the reality of it had really set in. There were no tears, just words. There were no thoughts, just impulses. Before I knew it, we had hung up.

Had I just called Tracy?
Did I tell her my mom died?

Did my mom actually die?

What did Tracy say when I told her?

My mind was filled with a flurry of confused thoughts and aimless questions. I couldn't grasp what was even happening.

A few minutes later I got a text from Tracy,

"Me and Alesia are driving over."

I replied, "Yall don't need to do that. Madeline and her husband will be here to get me soon."

Alesia is one of my other best friends. I met her through acquaintance because she was always a good friend of Tracy's. She'd come stay with us in Clemson occasionally which is when I really had the opportunity to get to know her. Alesia is another one of those genuinely good friends to have in life. She's always had an air of mystery about her. She's thoughtful, intuitive, who I'd consider to be the most composed of our friend group. There's a lot about her that I've always admired. She's got a more quiet form of confidence—she doesn't have to be the loudest in the room to make herself heard. When she talks, people listen. Her beauty and style are very classic, effortless. That's how I'd describe Alesia—she's a classic. She's another one of those friends who always shows up when you need them. Even when you think you don't need them to show up.

Tracy and Alesia showed up at my doorstep not even 15 minutes after that text. I'm not sure how they made it over as quickly as they did. Plus it was late and it was cold and we—I mean they—had to work the next morning. I felt bad for the inconvenience I had caused by startling them in this way. None of us had any words. What words do you even say to someone that just lost their mom so suddenly and unexpectedly? Literally minutes before we were standing there.

We stood out there in front of my apartment door in disturbing silence. I remember it was chilly enough to see our breaths in the cold air. They were in just as much shock as I was. None of us knew what to do or what to say. So we just stood there in that silence. There was nothing they could do for me but be there with me and that's exactly where they were and where I needed them.

Madeline and her husband pulled up to my apartment within 10 minutes of Tracy and Alesia getting there. Our silence was cut short.

I remember telling them, "I'm sorry you drove all this way for such a short amount of time. Especially when yall have to be at work in the morning."

"We're so sorry. We love you. Keep me updated." Tracy replied.

What a silly thing to apologize for, given the circumstances. What I would've given to be in their shoes, tired at work the next day from driving over to a friend's house who lost their mom the night before. Not that I'd wish what I was going through on them. I would've just much preferred to be in their shoes over mine.

They hugged me goodbye before they got back in their own car. I loaded my two dogs and a small bag of clothes with who knows what into the backseat of their trailblazer. I know one thing for sure, I definitely didn't think or remember to pack a black dress, an outfit for my own mom's funeral, as I was throwing things into my duffle bag that night. I know that because I remember having to go out and buy a black outfit a few days later with my dad and sister. And I specifically remember that because of how surreal it felt that life had just continued on for everyone around us. People were just out leisurely shopping as if their world hadn't just flipped upside down like my own. It was one of the strangest feelings I've ever felt in my life.

It was an eerily quiet hour-long drive from my apartment in Columbia to my parents house in Williston. Most of that drive was back roads. This meant there was very little sign of life outside of that in our own car and an occasional deer crossing the road in front of us nearing 11:00 p.m. on a Wednesday night. I don't remember a single word said between the three of us on that drive. I just remember sitting in the backseat, hugging my dogs tightly, praying there was some sort of misunderstanding that we'd be relieved to hear when we finally got to their house.

When we finally pulled into my parents' driveway, there was an unusual sense of peace. It would've appeared to be an ordinary Wednesday night for anyone that drove by—at least by that point in time. It was probably the complete opposite of calmness not long before our arrival. Whatever tragedy had unfolded two hours earlier left no residue to be observed as we pulled into that pebbled driveway. The same driveway that had recently been outlined by tens of beautiful blue hydrangea bushes the summer prior. My mom's favorite flower.

I could see the lights were on in the house which surprised me for some reason. I guess it was the striking contrast to the darkness in all the houses around us. A darkness I envied. A darkness that meant everything in their lives was normal that night. They could all sleep soundly. A darkness of theirs that was temporary and would end with the morning's sunrise. Unlike ours. Our darkness was just settling in.

As soon as my dad saw our headlights shine through the front windows, he made his way to the door. I was already walking through the doorway as he was coming through it himself. A fluid motion of chaotic devastation. As soon as Madeline and I saw him and made contact, we collapsed immediately into his arms without saying a single word.

The three of us stayed there for a long time, clinging to each other like our lives depended on it, wrapped in a silence only broken by the sound of our sobs. We held on tightly, as if letting go would somehow make the pain worse. As if letting go would force us to return to the reality that was patiently waiting to invade the space between us as we stood there as one. Tears spilled freely—his, hers, mine—a flood of grief that felt too heavy to bear. As we stood there, time slowed down, stretched out, and for what felt like hours, we stayed there, suspended in a moment too heavy for words. In that embrace, we didn't have to say a thing. The ache in our hearts said it all.

I'll never forget the moment I looked over to the kitchen from the space we were occupying together there in the living room. I could see that there was still a candle flickering as it sat on top of the counter. I knew my mom would've been the one to light that very candle earlier that evening. I didn't even have to ask. The very spark she lit before she left this world still danced in front of me, faint but alive. It was as if a piece of her lingered just beyond reach—still near, still warm, still with me. I could feel her, I just couldn't see her. That very moment is when it hit me that I'd never be able to see her again.

20

madeline

From the moment my sister was born, premature and ten weeks early, she was delicate and fragile. When my parents brought her home from the hospital, they said she was covered in medical cords and hooked up to numerous machines. I had my second birthday less than a month before meeting her for the first time. Ironically almost exactly my daughter's age when she met her newborn twin brothers, our sons, for the first time.

My parents told me that I was fully potty trained before my sister was born but within a few months of her being in our lives and in our home, I regressed back to diapers. I'm sure that's common behavior with many first-born children when a new sibling comes along. Being forced to share attention with another tiny human for the first time in their life.

I remember seeing the movie *My Sister's Keeper* for the first time. It resonated with me deeply. Not that I was ever asked to give in the same ways as Kate Fitzgerald—ironically Kate also being the name of the older sister—but I always felt like an afterthought. I had not experienced any major health issues or brushes with death, unlike Madeline. It felt like because I had always been the strong one, the healthy one, the stable one, I was expected to figure it out.

From the very beginning, Madeline fought hard to take her very first breaths so I spent years of my own life fighting in my own ways. Mostly fighting to please and appease my mom and dad. I loved Madeline dearly. Of course I did, she was my little sister. That didn't change the feelings of force to be strong and independent while she was comforted and sheltered from the same storm I was also being weathered by.

I've had two therapists in my life and I've spent both of my introduction sessions explaining the dynamics of my family and our past. I've told this same story both times. If Madeline didn't want to do something when we were growing up, I did it. Not necessarily because I wanted to—in fact, I'm sure I *didn't* want to many times. But I was politely told to. My parents signed her up for piano lessons and she cried when the instructor walked into our house for her first private lesson. Five months later, I was sitting on a piano bench in front of a small audience playing my first recital piece. Madeline expressed interest in horseback riding lessons but was afraid to do them alone so they signed me up to do them with her. Someone had to do it and if it wasn't going to be her, it was me.

I danced, did gymnastics, played soccer, took piano lessons, rode horses, went to art camps, played in the band, cheered. From the moment I was legally able to work and have a job, I had two jobs. You name it, I did it. When Madeline first began talking and couldn't pronounce her Rs quite right, she was immediately signed up for speech therapy. She struggled with math in high school so my parents had a private tutor come to our house weekly to help her learn. If something challenged her in any way or they saw her struggle in the slightest degree, they did anything within their power to provide an immediate solution. On the other hand, for me, I worked incredibly hard for my A/B honor roll. I cried over every single one of my A-'s and B+'s. I wanted to be perfect for them. I wanted to make them proud. Everything I did was *for* them. I wanted nothing more than to make them proud to have me as their daughter. Proud to be my parents.

Now that I'm a parent myself, I can confidently confirm those hobbies weren't all intended for me. There's no way I'd be given so much more opportunity than my sister for extracurricular activities. If she didn't want to do it, I did it and that's just how it worked for us. I don't resent them or her for this. If my tone here sounds bitter, it's a misconception. I'm simply intending to highlight the differences in how Madeline was raised in comparison to me. I was thrown into situations and expected to figure it out—to problem solve—as my therapist helped me realize. In many ways, by doing this, they created a more independent, resourceful person in me. I don't instinctively rely on others for a solution to a problem I'm capable of fixing myself. I don't see hardships as barriers—just inconveniences that may take a little time and effort to figure out.

As adults, it's clear that Madeline and I have grown into very different versions of ourselves—particularly in how we navigate pressure, face challenges, and make choices about the lives we lead. Though we came from the same place, our paths have unfolded in unique ways, shaped by different milestones and the individual ways we responded to the world we grew up in. She and I have never been particularly close, and I often find myself wondering if that distance stems from the way we were treated so differently as children. Though we shared the same house, the same rooms, and the same family, it sometimes feels like we lived two separate lives. We emerged from that world as two fundamentally different people. And when we each look back on those years under the same roof, we're staring at the same broken foundation—one defined less by warmth and safety, and more by the shadow of constant misfortune.

At 22 years old, Madeline married someone ten years older than her. None of us thought it was a good idea—especially not my mom. But she was in love and it was her decision to make. She was just out of college. She still had so much to learn about herself and about life. They did come out of that marriage with two precious little boys. The best things to come out of their time together, in my opinion. They're divorced now. It's not my place to share the details of that. He wasn't the man she needed or deserved though. We all knew that, long before they said their vows.

My mom was drugged up on my sister's wedding day. November 30, 2014. She always had a very specific look about her when she was high—glazed over, foggy, removed from herself. She was there but she wasn't. Her body was there but her mind wasn't. I still find it hard to describe what "high" for her meant. I guess it's because there was a lot more to it than just *that*. I knew my mom better than anyone. We were connected in ways that went beyond words, so I picked up on things others might've missed—subtle changes in her voice, the way she moved, even how she blinked. I could sense when something was off, even before she said a word.

I remember thinking that morning while we were getting ready in the bridal suite, "Seriously? You can't go ONE day without those stupid pills? Such an important, significant day and it's not meaningful enough for you to just be YOU for just one day?"

It wasn't that easy for my mom, I know that now. If it was, she would've been sober that day. Her girls, us, my sister and I, we meant everything to her. If it was that easy, she would've been fixed by those two weeks in rehab. If it was that easy, all of the tears, hurt, and heartache she'd caused would've been in the distant past. I know it wasn't that easy for her. If it was, she would've done it.

I was a lot more patient with her by this point in our lives. I'd had the luxury of going away to Clemson by the time my sister got married. Madeline didn't move away for college. She lived at home with our parents for most of those four years which meant she was around for the majority of it. It was very apparent to me she had grown resentful towards our mom as a result of being in the middle of all of it She talked down to her, picked fights with her, had just flat out lost all respect for our mom. It was very obvious any time I was around them. Her being like this on Madeline's wedding day was the ultimate slap in the face.

My dad sobbed like a baby their entire father daughter dance. He and I danced to the same song on my wedding day five years later. *Butterfly Kisses* by Bob Carlisle. It didn't take long for Madeline to join in with tears of her own. They had that effect on each other—if one cried, the other cried too. It was as if the rest of the room disappeared as they slowly moved across the dance floor. What they had been through together as a father and daughter was devastating. They had been each other's lifelines in the years since I had left for college while my mom was at her very worst. You could feel the despair as they clung to each other tightly, pleading unspoken words that only they could share in that moment.

"I wonder if he'll cry like this at my wedding?" I thought to myself. As if that was the only takeaway I had from those moments in time.

I didn't think much more of their dance beyond that. At least not at that point in time. I was just pitifully single at my little sister's wedding. I felt sorry for myself. Plus Madeline was always my dad's baby. He didn't want to give her away. Especially not to that guy.

But now, when I look at the photos from their father-daughter dance with an entirely different perspective, I don't just see a touching moment—I see heartbreak etched into every tear streaming down his face. He was carrying a weight far heavier and already grieving on levels much deeper than any of us could've possibly imagined or understood. If we only knew that day what was in store for our already hurting family just a little over a month down the road.

21

the eulogy

january 10, 2015

We held my mom's funeral service on Saturday January 10, 2015. Three short days after she left us here on this Earth without her. The days leading up to the service were strange and uncomfortable. I remember the morning after she died, waking up in my room in their house in Williston. A room I never actually spent more than a couple nights in at a time because I had already moved out by the time they moved into that house. But my mom still wanted me to have my own room. It was important to her for me to know I always had a space of my own and a place to call home. When I woke up in my bed in that room the next morning, I remember almost immediately realizing that the news of our devastating loss was going to have to be shared with the rest of the world. I wondered how to go about sharing that kind of news—the right words to use knowing it would be breaking news to many.

Here's what I shared in a Facebook post the morning of

January 8, 2015:

"My mom was my biggest fan, my best friend, and the best person I have and will ever know. Please keep my family in your prayers as we go through this extremely difficult, unimaginable time. Mommy—I'm going to miss you so so much and cannot even begin to fathom a life without you. Rest in peace and may angels lead you in."

Responses from both acquaintances and loved ones poured in:

"I believe I only met you once but when I worked at the hospital, your mom always talked about you... She said the reason she gave me a job was because I reminded her of her daughter. She was an incredible woman and truly of the kindest supervisors I have ever had the pleasure of working with. Just know that she was very proud of you."

"Love you sweet girl. Keep dancing, your mom will always be watching over you. She was such a wonderful woman and mother, I was honored to know her. Such a beautiful precious family."

"As long as her girls live—she will be for all of us to see. I remember Kellie when she was in college and working for me. A delight to be around and work with. She simply never changed from that. Will truly miss her."

There were so many emails, text messages, phone calls, and Facebook messages like this. It was clear to see she was loved by so many.

The morning after she died, my dad got a call from the funeral home staff stating they had completed the autopsy.

This was standard procedure given the nature of the situation with it being unexpected with an unknown cause of death. They asked if we wanted to come see her one more time before she was cremated. Apparently she wanted to be cremated. It was something she and my dad both decided at some point in time as both of their preferences. My dad respected her wish.

The thought of seeing my mom laying on a cold metal table in a lifeless body sent shutters down my spine. I told him I didn't want to go. I didn't want that to be the last image of her in my mind. The last time I saw and touched my sweet mommy. He seemed to understand—or at least I hoped he did. He said he did.

My sister agreed to go with him to see her one more time. They said I made the right call not going. The autopsy was invasive, she was cut apart and pulled back together in various areas of her body. Not going and seeing her like that is a decision I will never regret.

We had to meet the funeral director on several occasions leading up to her service to plan out the details. I remember struggling to comprehend even having to care about the flowers, the order of the service, the songs and who would play them. I couldn't comprehend how we, of all people, were expected to have to make such ridiculous decisions under such difficult circumstances. I guess I never put thought into who actually makes all of the arrangements for their loved one's funeral. It only makes sense for it to be those closest to them. The ones hurting the most over their loss.

Nothing about the situation, sitting there in that funeral home planning out my own mother's funeral service, alongside my 48 year old dad and 23 year old sister, felt real.

News spread quickly of my mom's passing in that small little town of Williston. We had people coming to our house almost constantly. They brought food, shared their memories and condolences, offered prayers and support. You could tell a lot of them weren't quite sure what to say to us. You could feel it most when conversation came to a lull. They weren't sure if it was a sign to wrap up their visit and give us our space or to attempt to carry on in small talk and distraction. Those poor people. They were doing their best.

"Let us know if there's anything we can do."

"We'll be praying for your family during this difficult time."

"We are so sorry for your loss."

It sounds cliche but it really is all you can do or say as an outsider, a bystander, in a situation like this. There is quite literally nothing anyone can do to make that kind of loss any easier, to make it hurt any less. We simply had to grieve—that's all we could do.

We saw a lot of faces we hadn't seen in many years. The constant movement and change in scenery during the day kept us as distracted as we could be. The anticipation of dusk always loomed. When the sun would begin to set and visitors subsided for the day, we were left with just the three of us. In such an unusual, indescribable feeling of void.

My dad, sister and I spent a lot of time going through old pictures, high school yearbooks, reading the notes she and my dad wrote to each other while they were in college. Everything of hers was everywhere in that house. Her scent, her clothes, her makeup, her jewelry. But not her. It was so indescribably sad. Complete and utter devastation.

I picked up my mom's cell phone at some point the morning after she died and found a text from my dad that immediately broke my heart into a million more pieces. I took a screenshot of it and sent it to myself because I never wanted to forget it.

I WILL ALWAYS LOVE YOU! WAIT FOR ME IN HEAVEN. I WANT SO MUCH TO FEEL THE WARMTH OF YOUR HUGS. YOU ARE MY POOKIE. YOU ARE MY SOUL MATE. PLEASE READ THIS TEXT IN HEAVEN. COME TO ME IN MY DREAMS LIKE BRIAN DID. I NEED TO KNOW YOU'RE AT PEACE. STAY WITH ME PLEASE. YOU ARE SO LOVED. SLEEP WELL AND ALWAYS KISS ME GOODNIGHT.

He sent her that text on January 7, 2015 at 11:07 p.m., a few hours after she passed away. A desperate last cry for her peace, for her to stay here with him. His soulmate. He never thought life would really come to this.

"I need to know you're at peace",

"Stay with me please."

He loved her so much. These words spoke to his profound grief. Sadness that transcended even the deepest level of heartbreak. Losing her was so much deeper than a broken heart. It was agonizing pain, overwhelming defeat, undeniable hopelessness. Not only was I grieving the loss of my mom, I was also now grieving my dad's severely broken heart.

Something inside of me me decided it was my duty to provide the eulogy at my mom's service. In a way, it was my version of the text my dad sent to her the night she passed. I wanted her to know what she meant to me, the positive memories she left me with. I wanted one more shot at making her proud. I wanted everyone to know who Kellie Ingram was and what she meant to so many. I knew doing this would give me that opportunity.

The night before her service, I sat down at my dad's work computer and typed out the eulogy in one sitting. I might've read over it once or twice after I finished but that was it. It was the most authentic, heartfelt goodbye I've ever said.

I still have the recording from her service on a CD I keep stored in my desk drawer. I still listen to it every so often. When I get to the Eulogy section of the recording and hear my own voice playing back, I can still hear the hurt, the shock, the denial in each of the words I'm speaking.

I didn't cry a single tear at my mom's funeral, I don't know why. I felt tears coming at several points but always stopped them before they'd fall. I remember going up to the podium and seeing all of my best friends filling the chairs facing me to my left. On my other side, there were three chairs reserved for me, my dad, and my sister on the first row facing me to my right. It still felt strange being a family of three. I remember as I spoke, I could see my dad's shoulders bouncing up and down involuntarily. It was his body's best attempt at subduing the natural motions that come with sobbing. His face was red, he kept pushing his glasses out of the way to wipe the tears from his eyes. My poor daddy.

I refocused my attention to the piece of paper in front of me, took a deep breath in an attempt to calm my nervous, and reminded myself what I was standing up there to do. To give my mom a proper goodbye. Then I began with a quote my mom had in a frame which always sat on her bedside table.

"Love is that condition in the human spirit so profound that it allows one to survive and better than that to thrive with passion, compassion, and style."

-Maya Angelou

As I'm sure all or most of you know, I'm Kellie's oldest daughter, Kate. Almost 25 years ago she and Daddy brought me into this world and two short years later blessed me with my sweet little sister Madeline. With that, the four of us formed the everlasting bond of a family that would love each other unconditionally for eternity.

My mom grew up in her heaven on Earth, the mountains of Asheville, North Carolina with her two little brothers and my two uncles, Mike and Clay. Fortunately, my granddad's work forced them to move here to Williston, South Carolina where she met and fell in love with her high school sweetheart, my dad.

No words that I write could attest to the love that was shared between my mom and dad. It was more than just a marriage, it was abundant, passionate and real. It was the kind of love that is both beautiful and rare, the kind of love that will live on without end.

My mom was such a beautiful, amazing person on the inside and out. She never left the house without her bright red lipstick and spent almost every car ride perfecting her makeup which explains the mascara marks on almost every passenger seat visor mirror she looked into. She had a personality that could light up a room and a laugh that felt unnatural not to join in with her. No matter the troubles or struggles that a person carried along with them she only saw the good in everyone she encountered.

She was a strong woman and an admirable one at that. She stood by her beliefs and never backed down from any argument she knew she should win—especially with her lawyer husband. And of course I can't forget to mention her impeccable driving skills. If you weren't aware of her skill behind the wheel, here are a few quick stories to give you an idea.

When we were in high school, one job just wasn't enough for my mom so she decided to sell real estate on the side. Her first clients were a wealthy couple from Columbia. One day they all got into my mom's car to head towards the lavish house that would eventually become their home, my mom puts her car in reverse, and then backs right into her clients' beautiful Mercedes-Benz. She somehow managed to close the deal a few hours later. Only Kellie Ingram could pull this off.

Another one of her fine moments was within the first few days of her and my dad buying a brand new Honda Accord. She decided to take Lisa and Joy on a road trip to eat at a Greek restaurant in Columbia. As they are leaving the restaurant my mom backs into the only car in the entire parking lot. As she pulls the car forward, the entire bumper falls to the ground except for one part left hanging. The three innovators brainstormed ways to glue the piece back onto the car before they left but, as I'm sure you could've guessed, their arrival back home included pulling into the driveway with a dragging bumper.

A couple nights ago my dad, sister, and I opened boxes of old pictures and yearbooks from mommy's high school days. Her senior year of high school, she won the superlative for best all around and Miss Congeniality in the high school beauty pageant. Oh how accurate each of those were. We laughed at the pages that had written at the top "reserved for" for her three best friends Lisa, Joy, and Carol. There was also a page reserved for Mark, which was turned into a continuation page for Lisa and Joy's yearbook signings.

One of my favorite parts of getting older has been hearing the real stories of the glory days with Kellie, Lisa, Joy, and Carol. It's funny how the tale of four goody goodies slowly progressed into the truthful adventures of the Bad Girls Club.

My mom and I had been through a lot over the years—more than most mothers and daughters experience in a lifetime. We had our differences during my teenage years but grew to become the very best of friends. Over the last few days, I've been reminiscing on the friendship we built over these last few years. It seemed like the more time that passed, the more I realized how similar we really were.

Mommy, I will miss your touch, your smell, your comfort and your love. I will miss our car rides, lifetime movie marathon days, and your new love of selfies. I also knew that when I hurt, you hurt because every time I cried, you cried. I knew how proud you were of me because you never let a single conversation between us end without saying, "Kate, I'm so proud of you."

Well Mommy, I want you to know that I could not be more proud to call myself your daughter. I have you to thank for my courage and independence and though we never could've planned for this tragedy, you have prepared me to find the strength to get through it. I know you will live on through me and I will not let you down.

My mom would want me to thank each and every one of you for being here today. Though she would never want anyone to mourn her passing, she would encourage us to lean on each other for comfort and support.

It will never make sense to me why such a beautiful life was taken so soon but goodness did she make it meaningful while she was here. It makes my heart so full to see how loved she was by so many and I can only hope she touched each of your lives even half the way she did mine."

You could hear people from the audience crying in the recording as I walked away from the podium and found my way back to my seat. Right after I finished my eulogy, we played her favorite song at the time of her death, *Something in the Water* by Carrie Underwood. The irony in that being her favorite song and the nature of her death still bothers me.

22

the overflow drain

january 7, 2015

My mom loved taking baths. It's something I'll always remember about her. She'd spend over an hour soaking in her bath most nights. It was her happy place. She was also an avid wearer of makeup—never left home without it. Mascara and a bold shade of red lipstick were her staples. She'd always come out of her baths with mascara stains under her eyes from washing her face but not scrubbing quite hard enough. Almost every wash cloth we owned was stained with that bright red lipstick of hers.

She'd spend hours soaking in the hot water some nights. She had a high tolerance for heat because of those hot baths she took. I remember she'd come out of the bathroom wrapped in a towel and you could see red marks where her body had soaked for so long in the scorching temperatures.

My dad eventually had to install a tankless hot water heater to support her bath habits. Thankfully. That was the only chance of warm water for the rest of us when we were in town visiting. She'd fill the bath all the way up and instead of turning the faucet off, she'd keep it running but pull the drain stopper up to let some of the water out while it continued to pour in. I guess baths are more enjoyable if the faucet stays on the whole time. I get it, the still water loses its heat fairly quickly once the faucet is off. The sound of the flowing water is also a critical additive for the overall experience of relaxing in a bathtub.

I can understand her reasoning. In fact, now I do it myself. I guess the habit carried over to me. And truly, I never thought anything of it until my husband brought attention to how strange it was to do that—as opposed to just turning the water off. In my mind, it was strange to just let the tub fill up once and turn the faucet off. And then sit there in lukewarm water. I guess we all have our ways.

When my dad remodeled the hall bathroom of their house (the old schoolhouse) in Williston, the new bathtub had an overflow drain that caught my attention the first time I took a bath in it myself. I'm not sure what it was about this particular overflow drain that caught my eye but for whatever reason it did. Maybe it had a larger opening than most and helped me finally understand their purpose.

Overflow drains are secondary drains located on the side of the tub. They are designed to prevent water from overflowing if the faucet is left running for too long and the wastewater drain (the drain at the bottom of the tub) is also closed. It was practical with my mom's bathing habits. It made total sense.

At the time of her death, my parents were actually in the middle of "creating" their master bathroom. When they purchased the house, the first big project they tackled was adding an extension to the back of the house to create a new master bedroom suite. The master bedroom was finished fairly quickly but the master bathroom was another story.

The master bathroom was a project my mom had been pestering my dad to tackle for many months. She was tired of being confined to the small space of the hall bathroom. There was only so much privacy to be had in a bathroom that could easily be seen from the couch in the living room. There was a door with a lock, yes, of course. But there's no peace and quiet when you can hear every word of the nightly news playing on the living room TV sitting just twenty feet away from where you soak in your bath.

My mom was ready for her master bathroom. She had exciting plans for it—a big soaking tub with a beautiful chandelier, a walk-in shower, a two sink vanity, and a TV mounted to the wall that she could conveniently watch from her view in the bathtub. It was going to be beautiful. She had a knack for interior design. She was the visionary. She still loved this kind of stuff even in the peak of her addiction battle. She wasn't cranking out brilliant design ideas on her worst days but she was right there, back at it on her good days. But she had to rely on my dad to make it come to life. Manual labor doesn't happen overnight. Plus finding the time to do it was always a challenge.

Shortly after my sister got married, in November of 2014, she moved into an apartment with her husband. My heart broke for my dad when my sister moved out. When he was left with just my mom in the house. She was not the person he once knew. The person he wrote love letters to in college, the person he raised two daughters with, the person he vowed to spend the rest of his life with. His companion was gone. He spent most of his time alone these days. And while she was physically close by, she was gone in a mental sense. How sad it must be to feel lonely in the presence of your once soulmate.

These were the thoughts that depressed me, for my dad's sake. By these days, a "normal" text exchange with my dad looked like this:

Me: "hey daddy. how's mommy tonight?"

My dad: "slurry. fell asleep at the dinner table. hopefully tomorrow will be better."

Looking back, it's so sad to think that these conversations were our norm. That there was so much darkness in the context of what should be such a simple question. It's so sad that it was so normal for us that he knew exactly what I was asking about. What I worried over day in and day out. She seemed so unpredictable. Even worse was when she started to become more predictable. Predictable in the sense of things continuing to only get worse. Predictable in the sense that it became a waste of time to ask how she was doing because I already knew.

We were all so helpless, especially my dad. It broke me to see him hurt so much. So when I asked "how's mommy?" and hoped for a "she's good today" response, the real hope was for my dad to have a normal day with his wife. It wasn't even really about her being okay anymore. It was about him being okay. Because, if my dad could have a normal day with his wife, that meant that I could take a deep breath and relax, even for just a short time, from the constant worry over *him*.

What my dad witnessed the night of January 7, 2015 is trauma my mind and heart aren't capable of comprehending. I wasn't there when it happened. I've only heard about it, in bits and pieces over time because it's too difficult to rehash in its entirety, from him. I have flashbacks to that night as if I'm in my dad's body looking out of his eyes, experiencing each moment as he did. The flashbacks are so vivid for me it's as if I was there myself. And they are sad, disturbing, traumatic. Artificial "memories" from a situation I didn't actually experience that the imaginative part of my mind haunts me with. Maybe this is empathy at its core. I've always said I empathize to a fault.

On the night of January 7, 2015, my dad found my mom's lifeless body in the bathtub of their hall bathroom. The recently renovated one. The one they were using as a spare until the master was done. The bathroom with the door you could see while sitting on the living room couch. Just a few feet away from where he was sitting minutes before.

It was a normal evening, he said. She wasn't sober but she was sober enough to eat dinner with him that night. They had chili. A staple in our house in those cold winter months. After dinner they cleaned up and my mom lit a candle on the kitchen counter, as she always did, to diffuse the smell of food that lingered throughout the rooms for hours to follow. My mom loved candles almost as much as she loved baths. If you walked in our house and 5 candles weren't actively burning, something was wrong. I definitely inherited her love for candles.

After the kitchen was clean, my dad found his spot in the living room on their leather couch to watch the nightly news and whatever sitcom aired after. My mom gathered her pajamas and headed into the hall bathroom. Though it was just my mom and dad in the house, my mom was very prude. She appreciated her privacy and never stepped foot into the bathroom, for any reason, without shutting the door. My dad heard the faucet turn on as she began her nightly bath ritual and knew it'd be a while before he'd see her again. She loved spending extensive amounts of time soaking in the tub.

I'm not sure exactly how much time passed before my dad began to wonder why she was taking so long. It was normal for her to be in the bath for a long time but I guess there eventually became a question of concern over how long it was taking that night. He could hear the faucet running so she was definitely still in the bath. He wondered if maybe she had fallen asleep—it wasn't totally unheard of for her, especially recently, despite how obviously dangerous it could be.

He knocked on the door and patiently called for her. "Kellie?"

He was respectful of her privacy and always knocked before opening. No answer. It wasn't totally unheard of. Like I said, she would fall asleep sometimes. He would just have to wake her up and remind her again, as he always did, how dangerous it was for her to let herself fall asleep in the bath. As if she didn't know. She was an adult.

When he opened the door, he found my mom in the bathtub as expected. What wasn't expected was that she was sitting up but her body was slouched over and her face was completely submerged in the water.

My dad said that shock took over and everything that happened from that point on was a blur of involuntary panic and survival instinct. He turned off the faucet that was still actively running—effortlessly and continuously feeding the pool of water that now filled my mom's lungs. He grabbed her by the shoulders and shook her aggressively. He was desperately trying to wake her up. It wasn't totally unusual to find it difficult to wake her from a medicated sleep. But this was different, he certainly knew that much. Her face was submerged in water for who knows how long. Even in this state of shock he was capable of recognizing how different this was.

She wasn't waking up. No matter how many times he screamed her name, it wasn't loud enough. She wouldn't wake up. He needed to get her out of the bathtub. He pulled her soaking wet body onto the cold tile floor and proceeded to do what any human would do to try to save another human's life. He frantically pushed on her chest. He held her nostrils closed while breathing his own air into her mouth, frantically trying anything he could to save her. But nothing was working, nothing was changing. And that's when he slowed down enough to notice the unexpectedly cool temperature of her skin and the blue undertone in the color of her lips. He knew right then she was gone.

My dad said the EMTs arrived within minutes of him calling 9-1-1. They quickly confirmed what he already knew. Shortly after the coroner was called to the scene, he declared her time of death and her body was placed inside a black bag so that she could be carried through their front door for the very last time.

Not only had my dad just lost his wife. He had also just become the only surviving parent of their two daughters, me and my sister. He was going to have to be the one to tell his children, their children, that they'd never see their mom again. His world had fallen apart.

While all of this was unfolding, I was getting back to my apartment after dinner with coworkers. Not a clue in the world what my dad was going through back at their house. It was just a normal Wednesday night for me.

In hindsight, almost every dangerous situation she found herself in since her battle with addiction began involved her inability to keep herself awake and falling asleep involuntarily, regardless of what she was doing. Without even realizing it until it was too late, her long baths probably brought unspoken concern to all of us. We'd see her fall asleep sitting up at a movie theater, in the middle of church, sometimes she'd even nod off as she was driving down the road. In those situations, we were right there to yell her name and wake her up immediately. To save her, in a sense, by expressing irritation and concern over her irresponsibility and incoherence. A bath was certainly no exception as an easy place to drift off. The difference was no one would be there to save her. If only we knew then what we know now.

I can't help but think of the unfortunate irony of that overflow drain. Its purpose is to prevent water from overflowing if the faucet is left on too long. Without the overflow drain there to capture the overabundance of water pouring into the tub, the same water my mom unconsciously inhaled into her lungs would've been pouring onto the floor. The water would have theoretically created a loud splatter and seeped under the crack of the bathroom door to quickly form a river as it found its way into the living room where my dad laid close by on the couch.

I've read that after four to six minutes of breathing in water without resuscitation, brain damage occurs which leads to eventual death by drowning. Four to six minutes sounds so long for someone to be submerged in water. But also so short. It's all so relative. If the overflow drain wasn't there, would the water have flooded into the living room and caught my dad's attention within four to six minutes? Leaving time for him to find his way into the bathroom and wake her up before it was too late. I'll never know. It doesn't matter either way, the overflow drain was there, doing what it was intended to do. To prevent the tub from overflowing while my mom lost her battle with addiction.

23

the toxicology report

In addition to the autopsy, toxicology testing was also performed due to the nature of her death. In the toxicology report, the forensic pathologist wrote that it was determined that my mom's death was an accident most probably caused by drowning in her bathtub due to incapacitation. The mental impairment that caused her death was found to be caused by mixed drug intoxication (oxycodone and diazepam). The toxicology report indicated non-toxic levels of oxycodone, acetaminophen, tapentadol, diazepam, nordiazepam, oxazepam, temazepam, zopiclone, trazodone, quetiapine and carbamazepine.

The reference to non-toxic levels seems a bit ridiculous if you ask me. Especially when you follow it up with the unbelievable amount of medication found in her system at a single point in time.

I think back to that psychiatrist and his metaphorical reference to my mom's game of Russian roulette. The real game, not the casino version, involves spinning the cylinder of a revolver loaded with a single bullet, pointing the muzzle at the head, and pulling the trigger. As you pull the trigger, the hope is that the chamber's empty. It's an extremely dangerous game because of its obviously unpredictable, life-threatening risks.

Every time my mom indulged in those copious amounts of medication, it was like pulling the trigger and hoping the loaded chamber wasn't aligned with the barrel. The odds worked in her favor for many years. I wish she would've seen her survival—her mere existence here on earth after everything she'd been through—as a win. I wish she'd seen each morning she woke up as a gift and walked away from the game while she still had a chance. As a winner. But the longer she played, the more she gambled, the more risky it became. Losing was inevitable. It wasn't if, it was when. Her *when* was Wednesday January 7, 2015. The day I lost the most important woman in my entire life.

IV

Part Four

24

denial

I went back to my one bedroom apartment in Columbia the night after my mom's service. I remember the pain in my dad's eyes when I hugged him goodbye. I know he had to be surprised and confused by my leaving so quickly considering everything that had happened, everything we had lost. The trust was, everything about that house in Williston overwhelmed me with the void of *her*. I couldn't get away fast enough.

It's difficult to know where to go next, to know what happens next, to figure out how to continue on, to move forward when you lose a critical figure, like a parent, so early on in life. At 24, I was beginning to build a life for myself but I still very much relied on the presence and love from both of my parents in so many facets. There is nothing that could've prepared me to lose my mom at just 24 years old.

I remember looking around me everywhere I went for several weeks thinking, "how is everyone just going on with life? I just lost the most important person in my entire world. Life will never be the same. How did time not standstill for everyone else too?"

It was the most bizarre and offensive feeling. A feeling I'll never forget.

In the days and weeks following my mom's death, I attempted to survive in the life I knew when I still had her. While doing this, I also went to sleep every night praying to a God I had never really wholeheartedly believed in, promising that I'd be the best version of myself for the rest of my life, that I'd never ask for anything else in the world if I could wake up tomorrow and have her back. I'd beg this of Him every night for many weeks. And every morning, I'd wake up with the disappointment of unanswered prayers. I couldn't accept that she wasn't coming back.

I did my best to go on about my life. I had no other choice. I continued dating the same guy I met just a few weeks before her death, jumped back into my stressful and exhausting job in IT, went out on the weekends with friends. None of it felt right. Everything felt out of place.

I'll never forget the first conference call I joined at work the Monday immediately following losing my mom. I worked and still work in the production support side of IT. This means that my area of work is focused on fixing broken things. We had something broken early that Monday morning so the first thing I had to do when I got to my desk was jump on a conference call with a bunch of other people. I remember anticipating comments of sympathy, coworkers asking how I was doing, passing along their thoughts and prayers. But I joined that call and no one said anything to me about it. Everyone was focused on the problem they were trying to fix. The only time I was addressed by anyone on that call was about our work. It was so strange.

"Everyone on this call sounds like they're just going about their normal lives. As if nothing has changed. How is this happening? Is life really just going on as if my mom didn't just die?" I thought to myself.

This is when I was smacked in the face with the reality of the fact that my life wasn't going to just stop. What happened to my mom was real but I had to keep moving.

I'll never forget one of my team members walking over to my cube later on that day. My first day back at work. I could tell he was hesitant to walk over but that he cared enough to push past the discomfort. He too had lost his dad at a young age.

He stood behind me and softly said, "I'm really sorry about your mom. I lost my dad several years ago myself. I can't believe you're already back at work but let me know if I can do anything."

I remember thinking, "Where else would I be if I wasn't at work? It seems like everyone else has moved on with their lives. Shouldn't I?"

The nights out with friends were different after losing her. I'd drink more than I could handle and sob out in public, in front of my friends and total strangers. I remember we went to the St. Patty's Day celebration in Five Points to celebrate my 25th birthday. It was just two short months after my mom died. In almost every picture from that day, my eyes are clumped together with mascara and practically swollen shut from crying the entire day. I was wasted and I was depressed. I remember nothing from that day. All I know is I woke up on the floor outside of my bedroom in the apartment I was living in with three other girls. No recollection of how I got there.

I picked fights with that guy I had just started dating over ridiculous things every time we'd go out. I wasn't myself but he hadn't known me long enough to know how impactful losing my mom was on my personality, my emotions, my reactions to situations. All he knew was that he had somehow ended up dating a crazy girl. I'm sure he felt stuck because he couldn't just dump the girl that had just lost her mom. What kind of asshole would that make him. I think I almost scared him away several times in those first couple months. Until I finally got hold of myself and he could see the real me again. The version of me he only knew for a couple weeks before my mom died.

Don't worry, we did end up having a good run together. We dated for a little over a year before he had to move out of state for work. What we had was only lust. It wasn't going to withstand the challenges of long distance.

For many months after my mom died, I would dwell on every picture, video, text message, voicemail, note, card, Facebook post, anything in my possession that gave me a piece of *her*. Her handwriting and the way she wrote 'i love you -Mommy'. I'd watch her throw her head back and listen to her sweet laugh in videos I had of the two of us saved on my phone. I'd laugh to myself over typos she never fixed in statuses she'd post on social media. I wanted all of it. All the things I couldn't have cared less about and never thought twice about while she was here with me. All these little things became treasures, sacred artifacts of her prior existence.

I'll never forget my first piece of good news I got at work after my mom died. I don't remember exactly what it was—a role change, a bonus, a raise or something. Something that made me proud and excited. As I was walking out of work that afternoon with my head held high, I got out my phone, went to my Favorites, and clicked "Mommy". It wasn't until I put my phone up to my ear to hear a ring that my heart dropped into my stomach.

"Your call has been disconnected because the number you dialed is no longer in service."

I had genuinely and briefly forgotten that she was gone. It had been several weeks and I was still very much in the thick of grieving her but the habit of her being the first one I wanted to call to share my good news was still there. It was a moment I'll never forget. It was the first time I recognized the gaping hole she'd left in my life. I realized in that moment that I'd been in a state of denial.

A month after my mom passed away, my dad decided to go on a trip to Peru. It was a work trip. A work trip he probably would've passed up at any other time to stay close to my mom but now the timing seemed opportune. Almost like destiny. He needed to get away. So he told his boss he'd go, extended his stay to be able to sight see and take advantage of his time there, and then he was on his way to South America.

I'll never forget how worried I was over him that entire trip. His first venture alone, across the world, as a widowed man. I remember him messaging me on Facebook about how sad he was when he got back to the hotel room the first night. He told me he couldn't stop crying. That he couldn't believe she was really gone. That he was taking a bath and drinking wine. He wasn't a wine drinker so that was somewhat abnormal. I wondered right then if I'd spend the rest of my life now worrying over my dad instead of my mom.

It was a mental toll I'll never be able to put into words. I don't know if it was the loss of one parent that created this intense fear of losing the other or if he really was just so depressed—so broken—that my worries were justified and made sense for anyone in my shoes. Not many people knew the depth of love my dad had for my mom the way my sister and I did. And without an understanding of that depth of love, it's not possible to fathom the impact of her loss on him.

All the years my mom was living in the predictable pattern of her unstable career—or whatever you want to call it, it wasn't really a career at that point—my dad never stopped celebrating each new job offer she received. It didn't matter to him that the circumstances of getting the new job were because she lost the prior. Well, I'm sure it *mattered* to him, but he never stopped celebrating her wins. He'd take her out shopping to pick out a new wardrobe and and then help her decide which of her new outfits she'd wear on her first day to work. He always made the small victories a big deal. He wanted her to feel proud of herself. He wanted her to succeed. He knew she could because she'd done it before. He held onto hope that each new job, each new wardrobe, each new first day and fresh start was her chance to start over. He never gave up hope for her. He never stopped cheering for her. That's the kind of love my dad had in his heart for my mom.

Not a single day went by for me for many years without worry over my dad. I think Madeline felt similarly but she had the benefit of a husband and her own children to distract her. I obsessed over his every move, his mood, what restaurant he was going to venture out to alone that evening. If he didn't answer his phone the first time I called, it sent me into a panic. I'd immediately spiral—asking myself if I thought there was a chance he'd ever give up on his own life. It was devastating to think about.

I'm not just throwing around the word "panic" when I use it. When he didn't answer his phone, when I couldn't get ahold of him immediately, it truly sent me into a state of genuine hysteria. My therapists told me it was PTSD from the night my mom died, no one answering our home phone while I was stuck in a state of unknowing and assumption. His loneliness killed me. And I knew he was lonely long before my mom died but being physically alone after tragically losing her was so different. With the worry over my mom's well being removed from my focus, I realized how many years of my life I had actually spent worrying just as much over my dad.

My dad stopped by my apartment when he got back in town from Peru and I'd never been so happy to see him. He brought me a few souvenirs that I still cherish so much to this day. They are more than keepsakes from Peru for me. They are reassurances and reminders that he always planned to come back to us. He bought that hand woven cardigan and handmade earrings for me because he wasn't planning to leave this earth the night he was messaging me from the bathtub in Peru telling me how devastated he was. His plan was always to come back to us. And he did. He just needed to get away from all of it for a little while. There was comfort in denial.

25

anger

Within a few months of my mom's passing, my dad put their house in Williston up for sale. I didn't blame him one bit. I can't begin to fathom how difficult it was to stay in that house, to pass that hallway bathroom tens of times a day, for even as long as he did. Everything in that house was her. Every paint color, the placement of every piece of artwork and framed family picture, every candle, the knickknacks. She was everywhere.

My dad asked me and my sister to come into town while he was packing up the house so we could help go through my mom's belongings. He wanted us to take what we wanted and he'd donate the rest. He wasn't exaggerating. He really wanted *nothing*. My dad got rid of *everything*. The art projects and school papers of ours that my mom held onto for 20+ years, the home videos of birthdays, Christmas mornings, and graduations, their high school yearbooks. He claimed he didn't want to tote all of it around with him.

"I don't want the clutter. I have no use for it."

We knew the real reason. He'd never be able to move forward if he carried everything behind him with him. I had a hard time with this - it was one of the first times I remember thinking, "this would make mommy so sad if she were here".

For the first time since she passed, I felt angry. Angry that it seemed so easy for him to dispose of our entire lives. Angry that my mom would do this to us in the first place. Angry that she would put my dad in the position he was in to even have to part ways with every item of her belonging. It was cruel, really. To leave the three of us here the way she did. But it didn't stop me from feeling sad for her. If there was a heaven up there and she was really watching down on us, she would've been deeply saddened to see all of our stuff go.

So for her, I took multiple boxes of things I'll never look at or touch again—possessions that were never meant to be mine. All the things my mom kept for herself. Little pieces of our past. Pieces of our childhood. She kept them for *them*. Our elementary school art projects, Christmas ornaments we made at a YMCA winter camp, medals I won at horseback riding competitions, boxes and boxes of dance trophies. All the "things" I'd keep of my own children's, for myself and my own sentiment, but would never expect them to want for themselves in their adult lives. But I just couldn't let them go. I had to keep them for her. So all of those things were packed in boxes and have moved with me five or six times since. They've always taken up an unreasonable amount of space in every attic they've occupied and probably always will because I'll never let them go.

Before he'd even officially sold the house in Williston, my dad moved closer to the coast. He bought a house on Folly Beach, located on the outskirts of Charleston, SC. It was another fixer-upper. Except this one was a short five minute drive to and from the beach. It was a cute little beach bungalow with a lot of potential. I think he committed to such a large undertaking so soon because he needed a distraction.

It was surreal watching him renovate and design that house entirely on his own. It was beautiful, no question about it, but I remember thinking how much of my mom's touch it was lacking. It was very minimalistic. It didn't have that "homey" feel she was always so good at creating. It was easy to see the eye he was lacking without her.

With the exception of my time in Clemson, this was the farthest away my dad had ever lived from me. It almost felt like it was his desperate escalate. His best attempt at a new beginning. His first step at starting over. I went to visit him as often as I could but it was hard with two dogs and a full time job. Every time I went to see him, it made me even more sad for him. He had figured out a way to build a new life for himself but it was a lonely life. He made a few friends with his neighbors but they were much younger than him and had lives of their own. He would go out to eat by himself often. His only companions were his two dogs, Rusty and Riley. I was so sad for him. I knew how lonely he was. It made me sad to be with him—to sit in an unfamiliar house on the leather couch he and my mom had picked out a decade prior. The beautiful circular kitchen table my mom talked him into buying right before she passed away. It was all very sad. I resented her for doing this to him.

My sister wasn't able to visit him much either. Archer was still an infant and it just wasn't ideal to travel multiple hours away with a young child in tow. I think one of my dad's hopes of buying a house near the coast was an enticing place for us to visit him. Life got busy though and that didn't happen like we all wanted it to. Once the Folly Beach bungalow renovation was complete, he found a house as close to both of us as he could and he hasn't drifted that far away since.

I've found that most of what I believe to be my form of anger in this grief I still live with has been centered around the sadness and sympathy I feel towards my dad. It angers me that he stuck by her side and held onto hope for so many years—he sacrificed his own sanity, his own happiness in hopes that he would be enough for her to want to get better. She had drained every ounce of energy, light, hope, desire from him. It wasn't her intention but she drug him down with her. He gained weight, he was irritable, he cried often. He no longer found joy in gardening, in fixing things, in doing the things that had always made him happy. But he vowed, all those years ago, to stand with her in sickness and in health and he wasn't going to walk away on that promise. So he gave and gave and gave until he had nothing left to give. And that's when she left him. She forced him to endure the most unimaginable, excruciatingly brutal form of heartbreak, the loss of his spouse, when his heart was already severely broken. When all he ever did to her was *love her.*

When I think about it like this, it feels like she kicked him when he was already down and from that perspective, it's hard not to feel angry.

26

bargaining

My mom called me on Saturday January 3, 2015 at 1:07 p.m.. Four days before she passed away. This is what she said in her voicemail:

"hey sweetie, I was just trying to catch up with ya. I wanted to see how you were doing health wise and just um hear your voice. give me a call when you get a chance. I love you. bye"

I've listened to that voicemail hundreds, if not thousands, of times since we lost her. I still have it saved on my phone. I never did return her call and it will always be one of the biggest regrets of my life. It's easy, at 24, to not understand how precious every ticking, unpromised moment in time is. At 24, when you've experienced close to zero loss in your life, it's simple to assume you have tomorrow. And another day. And another.

She asked me to call her when I got a chance. I know how many of those chances I had in the four days that followed. How did I not see how fragile and precious every single day of her life was given the magnitude of her addiction? To this day, I often wonder if I ever would've called her back if things had played out differently. If I had more than four days left on the clock of her life. Would I have called her back or just waited until she called me again and answered if it was convenient to me at the time?

I carried this bitterness inside of me towards her for the hurt she caused in our lives for so many years but I never stopped loving her. I know now that I'd give anything to go back to January 3, 2015 and answer that phone call.

What if it completely changed our trajectory. What if talking to me one more time was enough for her to flush those pills down the toilet. What if my voice could've acted as a reminder of what was truly most important to her in life. I had no idea it'd be the last time I'd ever hear her voice. The last time I'd hear her say, "I love you". The last time anyone will probably ever call me "just to hear my voice."

I'll spend the rest of my life wondering "what if" over all the things I could've done differently, said differently, handled differently that may have completely changed everything.

What if I went back into that visitation room at the rehab facility and told her how proud I was of her for being there?

What if I took her up on her offer and we had more girls weekends in my apartment in Columbia? What if more time like that gave her opportunities she was missing to see the true joys in life?

What if Papaw John hadn't died so suddenly? Was she trying to cope with that loss?

What if I flushed those pills down the toilet every time I thought about it? Would it have forced her to figure out how to survive without them? Maybe by doing that, she would've realized how much better life could be.

In quantum physics, the Many-Worlds Interpretation says

that every quantum decision spawns a new version of you in a parallel universe. If that theory is true, somewhere in another universe, I'd be able to see how each of those what if's played out. Maybe somewhere far, far away, everything turned out okay.

27

depression

Soon after my dad moved closer to us, I moved out of my one bedroom apartment and into a townhouse in the town center of Lake Carolina. While I lived there, I'd go on long runs in the evenings after work. Harborside was where I always ran. It was just one street over from my townhouse. I always felt safe running in there, regardless of the time of day. Every day, I'd run past the green house and the red house on my two mile route. It was such a bittersweet feeling to be so close to those two homes of ours.

I wasn't in a relationship for most of the time I lived in that townhouse. The guy I was dating when my mom died moved out of state shortly after I moved into the townhouse and we broke up a few months after that. I didn't mind being single but it was a bit lonely. I was always the relationship-type.

In the summer of 2016, my sister had just had her first son Archer. When I went to the hospital with my dad the day he was born, one of my brother-in-law's good friends was in the room visiting as well. I don't remember how we started talking or what it was about him that interested me. He wasn't my type—he was a blue collar worker, said he worked two jobs. Occasionally helped his mom with paint jobs but primarily worked in maintenance for a local school. Hourly jobs. Totally different from what I did and what I was used to.

Looking back, I have no idea what it was about him that drew me in. I think maybe I was lonely—even though I didn't realize it at the time. He was someone new and different. Rough around the edges.

He drove me back to my sister's house from the hospital that afternoon. I needed to get back to my dogs in Columbia and it was about an hour drive from Rock Hill where my sister lived. We sat on the back porch at my sister's house and talked for a little while. He smoked a cigarette and told me he had a 10 year old son he shared custody over with his ex-wife. We exchanged numbers and I got in my car and drove back to my townhouse in Columbia.

We started texting that first night we met. I don't remember all the details of how things unfolded but texts turned into phone calls which turned into double dates with my sister and her husband which turned into officially dating. I let him talk me into moving to Rock Hill even though my job and all my friends were in Columbia. My life was in Columbia. I told myself it would be worth it to live close to Madeline so that I could help with Archer when she needed it. She seemed to be doing most of the care taking anyway so I figured she could use some extra help. Plus she didn't have my mom around—I couldn't imagine how hard it was for her to become a mom so soon after losing our mom.

I'll never forget the night they told us they were expecting. My dad and I were at Red Robin eating dinner with Madeline and her husband. We were oblivious of the news they'd be sharing. It was only a few months after they had gotten married. Madeline was only 24 years old. We were wrapping up dinner and my dad asked for the check. Instead of bringing the check out, the waiter had a hand full of cupcakes. My dad and I looked at each other in total confusion. It wasn't anyone's birthday. Did they come to the wrong table?

Madeline caught on that we weren't figuring out the subtle hints and I could see that her face was turning red. She always blushed easily when she was embarrassed or nervous.

"Yall!!! I'm pregnant!!!!" She said with irritation in her voice.

It was like the white cupcakes topped with birthday sprinkles should've easily given it away.

I looked at my dad and he immediately burst into tears. I still don't know if those were happy tears or sad tears. I think they were sad tears, for many reasons.

When I officially decided to make the move to Rock Hill, my dad helped me pay for the rental house which was only about 10 minutes away from Madeline's house. Rent was expensive in that area and I was still fairly early on in my own career. Definitely didn't have any form of savings to fall back on.

My relationship with this guy got more serious fairly quickly. He asked if he could move his stuff in since he was staying with me every night anyway. I wasn't against the idea. I enjoyed his company.

I drove back and forth to work in Columbia every day. It was a long commute and it was exhausting. Drew, the guy I was now sharing a house with, didn't work long hours so he was at my rental house a lot more than I was. It took a while for me to realize that it bothered me how much time he spent there without contributing anything to rent or utilities. I brushed it off and reminded myself that it was nice to have his company.

The longer we dated, the more toxic things became. He didn't have many friends of his own so he wanted to spend all of his time with me. It was flattering at first but almost made it difficult for me to find time to spend with my friends back in Columbia. The mere mention of thinking about making plans with them seemed to hurt his feelings. Without even realizing it, I began making excuses of my own to get out of plans with them. I'd still go as far as making the plans so that it didn't seem like pure avoidance—like I was hiding something (even though I was)—but then I'd back out of them. Eventually, every single plan I made I'd back out on. Because anything I tried to do with my friends, even the mention of making plans with them, would make him angry.

He wasn't the yelling type of angry. He was the shutdown and don't speak to you for days type of angry. But he still stayed in *my* house that he contributed nothing to. We'd just be two people, not speaking, living under the same roof. I hadn't even done anything to deserve to be treated the way he'd treat me. I'd never follow through with the plans I made because of how upset he'd get. Apparently I wasn't even allowed to think it. Because if I showed interest in keeping my friendships, that meant I wanted to be with my friends and not him and that just wasn't acceptable. One day I woke up and it hit me. I was an extremely toxic and controlling relationship.

I posted a picture on Instagram one day with two male coworkers who were also friends of mine. It was the day we graduated from a training program and we were holding up our certificates in the picture.

Drew saw the post, took a screenshot of it, and sent it to me saying, "I see what you're doing when you say you're 'working'. Ridiculous."

He didn't talk to me for a solid week after that.

I got to the point of feeling complete misery and dread around him. I would drive to work every morning with excitement to get away and drive home every evening with looming sadness. I was so unhappy but I was stuck. I didn't know how to get myself out of the situation I had gladly walked myself into. My friends stopped making plans with me and I honestly didn't blame them. Why would they keep trying? All I ever did was turn them down. I'd see pictures of all of them smiling at tailgates and weddings and my heart filled with sadness, anger, envy. I hadn't even realized how bad of a situation I was in until it was too late.

I remember I reached out to Tracy and Sammi one day and told them I wanted to plan a trip to New York City to visit Sammi. Sammi had moved back to New Jersey right after college graduation. I'm sure they were shocked to even get a text from me by that point. If they were, they didn't show it. They were good friends and they probably just wanted to take advantage of the opportunity to be with me while it was there. While I wanted to be with them. I dreaded telling Drew that I was going but this was my first attempt at an escape. And we did it. We went to New York. When I got back, he didn't ask me how my trip was or tell me he was glad to have me home. The only thing he did was shun me for the next four solid days.

After that trip, I started to find even more irritation in all the little things about him that always bothered me but I was too afraid to do anything about. The way he smoked in the car with the windows up, the way he carried a loaded Glock around with him everywhere he went in my house, the way he didn't help pay for bills but would buy new things for himself every time he left the house, the way *his* stuff took up so much of *my* space. All of it drove me crazy.

Soon after our trip to NYC, my friends invited me to an Eric Church concert. We'd been to many Eric Church concerts together. He was one of our favorites.

"Of course!" I told them, as butterflies filled my stomach knowing the reaction this would evoke from Drew back at home.

I told him when I got home from work that day that I was going to the concert. It turned into the biggest fight we had ever gotten into. Probably only because I never stood up to him. I never did the things I really wanted to do. I only ever did the things he wanted me to do so there was never a reason to fight until that moment. This was the first time I genuinely felt physically scared in his presence.

"You're so selfish. All you care about is yourself. Everything is always about YOU and what YOU want. I can't believe how terrible you are." He screamed into the door of the room I had myself locked in.

I was sobbing into a pillow on the bed. All I wanted was to call my dad and ask him to come pick me up. What had my life become? A life I needed saving from.

About an hour later, I got a text from Drew telling me he was done and that he'd be back the next day to come pick up his stuff. When I was at work and didn't have to be around for it. Despite the unavoidable sadness of the situation, I felt a huge sense of relief. Immediate weight off my shoulders. I responded and asked him to leave his key when he came back the next day. That was the last time we spoke.

I remember I half expected to come home from work that next evening and see his Jeep in the driveway. He was manipulative. I figured he'd probably try to apologize or guilt me into fixing things. Fixing things would be me agreeing not to go to the concert. That's how ridiculous and controlling he was. I had already decided it wasn't going to happen. I didn't care how much he pleaded, I was done.

To my surprise, when I pulled in that evening, he wasn't there. All of his stuff was gone from inside just as he promised. The key was on the kitchen counter just as I asked.

I didn't sleep well in that house alone for the rest of the time I lived there. There was no question I was afraid of him. Afraid of what he may be capable of in a state of rage. It terrified me. I needed to get out of that place as fast as I could.

A few months later, I bought my first house in downtime Columbia. It was a cute little house that my dad helped me fix up. And I was right up the road from my best friends for the first time in over a year. Life was going to be better.

I went to a wedding in Hilton Head with Tracy and Alesia some time that first summer I was back in Columbia, 2017. It was the first time the three of us had gone away together since my breakup with Drew. I had high hopes it would be a weekend to remember.

One of our best friends in college was getting married so the reception was somewhat of a college reunion. It was weird to be around everyone again. I had missed out on so many football tailgates the prior football season because of the whole toxic relationship thing. I could definitely feel that all of their friendships had gotten stronger. I was no longer an insider. This was the first time I felt very much like an outsider with all the people I'd considered my closest friends.

Things were okay at the reception for a while but at some point, I started getting in my own head. I felt like Tracy and

Alesia were purposefully making inside jokes and talking about things they'd done that I wasn't apart of. It was unusual for me to feel this way around them. Like an outsider. Left out. The longer the night went on, the worse it felt—until I decided I couldn't take it anymore. I walked out of the reception hours before it ended unannounced, called a taxi, and went back to the hotel we were all staying in.

I expected an immediate text from someone asking where I was but didn't hear a thing. It was an unrealistic expectation—everyone was drinking and having a good time enjoying themselves at the reception. There were too many people to notice me disappear. But the more I sulked in my own misery, the more upset at them I became. I couldn't stay in this hotel room with them that night. Not only was I angry with them but I was embarrassed of myself. So I used my phone to find a different hotel with vacancy that night, grabbed my stuff from our hotel room, called another taxi, and was on my way.

The second hotel I stayed in was more of a beach-side resort. The only availability they had was a one bedroom condo which was more than I needed and could afford but I would make it work. When I went up to the welcome desk of that resort, the guy working at the front desk just happened to be a guy I knew. We had worked together in high school at the YMCA as summer camp counselors. Just my luck. I'd make a last minute reservation at a random resort at 10:00 p.m. on a Saturday night *by myself* and just happen to know the only person working at their office that late who was also going to have to check me in.

He was so excited to see me. Thankfully he didn't ask any questions like I was anticipating. Maybe he could tell I had been crying and didn't feel like it was his place to pry. I'm glad he didn't, I'm not sure what I would've said.

I'll never forget going into that dark and isolated one bedroom condo by myself. Far away from anyone or anything I knew. I had no car. Nothing on me but the small bag I had packed along with the dress I was still in from the wedding. I set my stuff down and laid in that random bed and cried. Not just occasional tears. Whaling cries.

Around that time, I got a text from Tracy asking where I was. She said they hadn't seen me in a while and were worried. I don't remember exactly what I said but it was enough for her to know that I was not myself. I was hurting. I was struggling tremendously. But also that I was safe.

I cried myself to sleep that night and didn't leave that bed the entire next day. I didn't turn the lights on, didn't eat. The only light I saw those 24+ hours was that from the TV that I had playing softly for background noise—it made me feel a little less alone. It felt like the longest day of my life. I don't know why I stayed there like that for so long. Why I didn't reach out to someone to come get me. Why I didn't once step foot out of that dark room of the expensive condo I stumbled upon late the night before.

I felt abandoned in that isolated condo. Abandoned by my mom. Abandoned by the friendships I had unintentionally but single-handedly destroyed. Abandoned by who I used to be. I had lost myself. I was, without a shadow of a doubt, severely depressed. This was my form of rock bottom.

I called my dad the following morning and told him what happened. He was surprised to hear that my friends would make me feel that way. He knew how good of people they were. I think he knew it was a lot deeper than that. That it wasn't them, it was me. But he didn't tell me that, he never would. He was always on my side. And just as he always did, he dropped everything he was doing and drove three hours to come pick me up from that one bedroom condo. I'd never been so happy to see a familiar face. He didn't ask any questions on the way home. We just talked as if we were driving home from Hilton Head under totally normal circumstances. We picked up Captain D's for dinner, ate so much fried food our bellies hurt, and then he dropped me off at my new house downtown.

"You need to text your friends and let them know you're okay. Tell them you're sorry for leaving." He pleaded with me as he pulled out of the driveway.

"Thanks for coming to me pick me up. I love you Daddy." I said and then turned around to go inside.

I didn't reach out to my friends immediately but I did eventually. I think that event put a damper on my relationships with them for a quite a while. Understandably so. Honestly, I don't remember when things eventually went back to normal with us or how we moved past that. I'm just glad they were able to move past it. To forgive me. To give me yet another chance to just be a friend. That's all they ever wanted from me.

Tracy says that it seems so blatantly obvious to her now that was my cry for help. That she wishes she had done more. That she'll always regret not doing more. She said she was too focused on going to bars, meeting new people, being in the social scene to comprehend what I was going through. The truth is, that's what most people our age were doing at that point in our lives. She wasn't a villain for continuing to live her life. It's not her fault my grief prevented me from being able to live mine.

There was nothing anyone *could* do for me. How could I be helped by someone else when I couldn't even help myself? I just had to work through it and get through it in my own ways and on my own time. This was my version of depression in grief. Until I met Steven.

28

steven

Steven and I got married on November 30, 2019. We were engaged for about a year and then dated for a few years after that. But we knew each other long before it all. I'll get to that later.

We chose Charleston, South Carolina for the wedding location because it felt like a good middle ground for the majority of our guests being from either Columbia, South Carolina or Savannah, Georgia. I've also always just loved Charleston. It's where my family used to go on day trips growing up and will always hold a special place in my heart for that reason as well.

Late November in Charleston was a risky selection with the unpredictable weather in South Carolina but we did it anyway. We visited a few venues in the area before deciding on the Carriage House at Magnolia Plantation. I think we both knew that this was very much Kate-chosen and Steven agreed-upon. He would've been fine driving up to the court house. In fact, I think if it were up to only him, that's exactly what we would've done.

The months of stress of wedding planning (for me, Steven

doesn't get stressed) was well worth it in the end. Our ceremony was set up right beside the Ashley River which ran parallel to the plantation. The weather was beautiful that day, sunny in the high '60s. It really couldn't have been any more perfect. We had wooden fold out chairs lined up for guests, three string musicians who played for both the ceremony and the proceeding happy hour, and reception programs with hand-drawn artwork of the Carriage House. Our wedding colors were gold, hunter green, and black which we used to drive the moody, romantic, intimate theme of the evening. It was beautiful perfection down to every last detail. I know my mom would've loved everything about it and to this day, it deeply saddens me she wasn't there to be a part of it.

Steven and I first met back in 2013 when I first started working for the company we are both still employed by today. He actually came to teach a segment of one of the technical training classes I was taking as part of their entry level training program. He was an insignificant figure in my life back, a stranger, but I still vividly remember meeting him that day.

Tracy had already been working for the same company for a few months when I got hired on. I remember texting her saying, "Do you know a Steven Lariscy? He's coming to teach one of our classes today."

She responded with, "Yes, I know Steven! He's a genius."

Maybe that's why my first encounter with him was unforgettable. I've always genuinely admired really smart people.

The class he taught was supposed to run a full half day but he only spent about 20 minutes with us before telling us he was done and we could leave or do whatever we wanted with the rest of the allotted time. This was an unusual treatment in these training program classes because we were being paid full salary to sit in class all day for several months. I guess Steven didn't care because he wasn't the one giving us our paychecks. I think all of us sitting in the class looked at each other with hesitation and confusion—no other instructor had given us an invitation to do whatever we wanted with the time not being used for instruction. I'm pretty sure we all just stayed in the classroom after Steven left. We were rule followers.

I remember being so intrigued by Steven. He was a genius according to Tracy but he was also so carefree, so relaxed—I could see that in my very first interaction with him.

I was still in that long term relationship with the guy from New York in August of 2013 when I met Steven for the first time. When we broke up in mid-2014, one of my coworkers got wind of it and immediately tried to set me up with Steven.

"Just go on ONE date with him, Kate!!"

"He is so great!! I wouldn't lie to you!" She'd tell me with any passing opportunity.

But I was utterly heartbroken and had no interest in anyone else. Steven and I crossed paths occasionally in our work over the years that followed but it wasn't often and the interactions were usually so short that we had next to no opportunity to really get to know each other—until August of 2016.

In August 2016, Steven and I were both asked to participate in our company's disaster recovery exercise on the night shift. The disaster recovery exercise was an unusual experience for everyone. We worked from an offsite location with a much smaller group of our peers who were also participating in the exercise. Since we were on night shift, our hours for the four days of the exercise were from 10:00 p.m.-10:00 a.m. It was brutal.

2016 wasn't the first time Steven and I had worked together

in this capacity but for some reason it was different this time around. I was more interested in him, I found joy in his company, his jokes were even funnier this time. I remember on the last night of our shift, I was sad for it to be over because it meant our time together had ended. We'd both be going our separate ways, working on different floors of the same building, guaranteed not to have a need to speak again for several months at least. I hated the thought of it. I didn't want to wait for another year to pass to be able to spend time with him again.

I looked for any and every excuse to text him. I could tell by his short and lacking, delayed responses that he was either not a big texter or not at all interested in me but I didn't let up. I knew he was more reserved than me and was probably completely oblivious to my attempted pursual.

I carried on about my life but I couldn't stop thinking about him. I sent him a text late one Friday telling him to have a great weekend but didn't hear back that night or the entire next day. Every new incoming text was met with disappointment when I realized it wasn't from him. I was so bummed.

Then, late that Sunday afternoon, I got a text from him saying, "I hate I'm just seeing this. I'm at my parents house for the weekend and usually put my phone away while I'm here. But it made my day to see your text. I hope you had a great weekend too :)"

I think this was the very moment I realized that maybe there actually *was* something there. I was ecstatic.

Steven and I hung out fairly often after that. I remember leaving a weekend getaway in Clemson with my friends a day early because he had invited me to come over and hang out at his house. We watched movies, talked about work, went out to eat, ordered food in. We did all the things couples do. I don't remember ever making it "official" so I guess it just organically became that. I remember the first time he told me he loved me, we both cried happy tears. It felt so good to be in love with him. My dad also loved him which was extremely important to me. Everything just felt so right.

Steven proposed to me in December of 2018 while we were decorating a Christmas tree in the house I owned and lived in by myself and my two dogs at the time. It was actually the second tree he helped me drive back to my house after deciding I didn't like the first one I picked out. I was completely surprised when he proposed. We had looked at rings a few months prior but I had no idea he bought one and no idea he had plans to actually propose. It was a dream come true. There wasn't a doubt in my mind that I wanted to spend every day of the rest of my life with Steven. He was my soulmate, I knew it.

Maren Morris released a song called "To Hell and Back" in 2019. The first time it came on the radio in my car, tears came pouring from my eyes. In the song, she says:

"You didn't save me. You didn't think I needed saving. You didn't change me. You didn't think I needed changing. My wings are frayed and what's left of my halo's black. Lucky for me, your kind of heaven's been to hell and back."

It was as if I wrote that song myself about Steven.

For years after my mom died, I was completely broken in so many ways I didn't even recognize until I met Steven and was able to see the sun shine again. I was depressed and reclusive. I distanced myself from my very best friends and the more they pushed to try to help me, to get me out of the isolated shell I had built over myself, the more I pulled away. I don't know how I didn't lose their friendships entirely in those years. I guess that speaks to real friends and what that actually means. They saw me struggling when I couldn't even see it myself. They tried to help and when I wouldn't let them, they stayed patient and continued loving me anyway.

My life had become a sad, black hole and I had settled into it. I was lonely even when I wasn't physically alone. I struggled to find joy in the moments and places that once brought me my highest highs. Happiness had become a figment of my imagination. A stranger I once knew in another life. I cried myself to sleep on random nights—sometimes I knew it was over my mom and sometimes I couldn't identify a specific reason. I was in full-fledged depression. Not a phase of depression, a life of it. I had lost myself and all the best parts of my personality, of what made me *me*. I didn't even realize how rock bottom I really was until Steven came along and unknowingly saved my life.

I imagine being in Steven's shoes is really hard sometimes. He never met my mom and all he knows about her are the stories I've shared and the tears he's watched me cry. We didn't really know each other when she passed away, though he did sign a card that got passed around our department when word got out that my mom died unexpectedly. What he knows now is all hearsay from listening to me talk about what I went through and how it impacted me. He definitely sees the aftermath of it, even ten years later. There have been so many random breakdowns, bouts of unexplained sadness and loss of joy that I eventually claim as depression, and uncontrollable tears over missing her.

It must be strange to be in his shoes. A fictional character that his wife cries herself to sleep over on random nights. A ghostly presence only spoken of but never seen, a familiar name he hears as stories are shared with family over the holidays, a face in pictures of a woman he will never know. A woman who mothered his wife and then left her. A woman whose blood runs in that of all three of his children. It must be so hard to be in his shoes. When I'm in those moments of deep grief, he knows there is nothing he will ever be able to do or say to fix it. Instead of talking, instead of telling me everything is going to be okay, he sits in silence and holds me until I let go first—because when I let go, he knows I'm okay again. He knows that he will never understand what all I've been through so he doesn't try to relate because he knows it wouldn't be fair to pretend. Instead he listens and never compares. He knows that a lot of my fragility, emotional response, anxiety, and depression is a result of the trauma I've experienced and he knows that we will never be alike in that regard. He knows all of this and he's still okay with it.

Instead of questioning my unpredictable, unexplained lows he admittedly will never understand, he recognizes when I start to slip into one and picks me up before I fall. He knows that holidays, birthdays, promotions, celebrations, big moments of joy in any regard will always be slightly overcast for me because of sadness over missing, needing, wanting my mom to be here too.

We both know that Steven will never understand *me* because such a huge part of me is *her* and he didn't know me when I had her. That's what I love so much about him. He doesn't try to make sense of my flaws, he doesn't try to fix all the parts of me I still see as very broken. He never tried to change me or save me because he never saw me as needing changing or saving. He asked me, as is, to spend the rest of my life with him because he loves me for exactly who I am.

STEVEN

There have been so many big moments in the life Steven and I have shared together that I wish my mom could've been here to experience with us. We have three beautiful children, Kinslee, Keaton, and Kole who have filled our lives with so much love and purpose. They've brought us to our knees begging for mercy in the most challenging times and lifted our spirits as high as the most distant clouds in the sky in the best of times. They embody the best qualities of me and Steven both—but they're also their own human. They make me want to be the best version of myself. They've each taught me patience, perseverance, and resilience I wouldn't have known if it weren't for them. The strength I saw in myself as a result of the life before them carries no weight to the strength I see in myself now as their mom.

I don't know if soulmates really exist or if the universe really does have a partner destined for every human being on the planet. Before Steven, I would've doubted it. The idea seems pretty far-stretched, unrealistic. What I do know is that every single decision, mistake, success, change, move, adjustment, chance, problem, fix, risk, all of it is what got me to where I ultimately crossed paths with Steven. When I look at it like that, I'm a little more okay with everything that happened before him.

This book is for you but it's also for me, for my children, for Steven. I never want to forget the promises I made to him on our wedding day. Storing them here feels like a promising place to help keep them alive.

Steven,
I want to preface what I'm about to say with one statement –

and that is that there is simply no way to stand in this moment right now and justly represent the depth of my love for you and everything you mean to me in these words.

Before I met you, I didn't know what I wanted in a life partner. I had this idea in my mind, of course, but I really only knew one thing to be true. I knew I wanted a love as faithful, as pure, and as precious as the love I witnessed between my parents for 25 years. I've experienced my own form of this kind of love because of you.

Since the very first day I met you, on August 23, 2013, I've been completely and utterly intrigued by you – your brilliant mind, your tender heart, your unwavering patience. What has always fascinated me about you is your complex assemblage of characteristics that make up the most simple, level-headed person I've ever met. I am so incredibly proud to be standing up here today to become your wife for so many reasons –

Your intelligence. Your intelligence was one of the first things that attracted me to you. But it wasn't just because you were so incredibly smart, it was because you were so incredibly smart yet so incredibly humble. You never use your intelligence to get ahead of others, to correct someone when you know they're wrong and you're right, to make it known that you are the smartest person in the room. You use your intelligence to help and teach others and to do the best job you can do. You use your intelligence to draw out complicated technical concepts on a napkin as we stand in the kitchen and you explain them to me because I insist on understanding right then despite the ten hour work day we've just gotten home from. I love that I get to spend the rest of my life learning from you.

Your patience. Your patience is what I admire most about you. I still don't quite understand how someone so passionate can exert so much patience, but I sure do love you for it. Your patience is what gives your intelligence its magnitude of positive impact. It's what makes you such an effective teacher and why others yearn to learn from you. Your patience is what gets you through all of my "5 more minutes" that turn into 2 hours and sharing a very small master bath and closet with me. Your patience is what will also make you such an amazing father to our children one day and what I will continue admiring about you every single day of our new life together.

Your heart. Your heart is what I love the very most about you. Your heart always puts family first, makes each and every one of your relationships important to you, and loves fully and unconditionally. Your heart is the love letter on the kitchen counter when I go to sleep before you on a work night, the "I love you" sticky note that you leave under my keyboard when you drop off breakfast and a redbull at my desk, it's also the proudness behind the high-five you give me every single time I get a jeopardy question right. Your heart is the reason I've never cried alone while sharing memories of lost loved ones during our late night back porch conversations – and your heart is to thank for drying up most of these tears and bringing so much light back into my life. I love that I will be loved by this heart of yours for the rest of my life.

Today, I want to make promises to you that I will always keep.

I promise to never stop holding your hand and to always give you a goodbye kiss before leaving for work.

I promise to give you all of the love and support I give Rocky.

I promise to always set the sleep timer, to never go to bed angry, and to continue trying to understand the purpose of and your love for Family Guy and Rick and Morty.

I promise to join your laughter with my own and when you can't look on the bright side, I will sit with you in the dark.

I promise to love, respect, protect and trust you, and give you the best of myself – for I know that together we can build a life far better than either of us could imagine alone.

I choose you, Steven. And I will choose you over and over, every day, for the rest of my life. I love you.

I still mean every word I shared with him that day and have fallen even more in love with him every day since.

29

acceptance

Losing my mom brought our family of three closer together than we ever were before. When everything broke around us, we clung to each other like lifelines. That kind of pain doesn't leave without leaving something behind—and for us, it was a deeper connection.

Life was extremely hard for all of us for many years. There's no question that it's still hard for each of us in our own ways. The difference time has made in my personal experience with grief is that it's diluted it, in a sense. It still comes in random waves but the waves are spread further apart and when they hit, they don't linger for as long as they used to. I've become more aware of what to expect, over time, so I'm able to brace for impact and bounce back more quickly than I used to be able to.

I avoided therapy for far too long. In hindsight, if I had addressed the issues head on as soon as I should have, it probably wouldn't have taken me quite as long to get to where I am today. When I finally either admitted to myself or was convinced by a friend or a loved one that I *needed* to talk to a professional, I quickly learned how traumatic much of my life has been. Counseling has helped me validate my emotional response to situations and the anxiety and depression I've struggled with for most of my life. It's also helped me make sense of and understand some of the things that have happened to me in the years following my mom's death.

I have a recurring dream that started a year or two after losing my mom. I have this dream about once a week and it's always a slightly different rendition of the exact same story. In the dream, I've lost touch with her but she still exists. She's still living—just living her own life that's not part of ours anymore. In the dream, it always starts by my learning that she's still alive and realize it's been months, if not years, since she's tried to reach out and speak to me. I wake up with tears in my eyes every time I have this dream. I always have the same feelings of betrayal and confusion. While dreaming this, I can't understand why my own mother would leave me, voluntarily lose contact with us—her husband and her own children. Each time I have this dream, it re-breaks my heart. When I brought this up to one of my therapists, she told me this is a telltale sign of unresolved trauma. I guess it makes sense.

My dad eventually met another woman. In 2020. The same year my daughter, Kinslee, was born. Her name is Amy. It was hard for me at first until I realized how good she was for all of us. She's gentle, kind, and laughs the sweetest laugh at all of my dad's jokes. She was a true blessing and she still is. For the first time in my entire memorable life, I don't go to sleep at night worrying over my dad. There's no way to quantify the amount of relief I've felt in my heart ever since she came into our lives.

As I mentioned at the start of this book, two short years after

Kinslee was born, she was joined by her twin brothers, Keaton and Kole. All K's was intentional. Kate, Kinslee, Keaton, Kole, and Steven (sorry Steven). It's okay, he just laughs about it. He says if we ever have a fourth (which we won't), their name will have to start with an "S". Otherwise, he'll be okay with being on his own. Steven was gracious enough to let me include a little piece of my mom's legacy in each of our childrens' names:

> *Kinslee Rose Lariscy - Kins-"lee" in memory of my mom, using her middle name "Lee".*
> *Keaton Lee Lariscy - Lee in memory of my mom, using her middle name "Lee".*
> *Kole Burch Lariscy - Burch in memory of my mom, using her maiden name "Burch".*

They don't know it yet but they'll always have a little piece of her in them. I hope they'll grow to appreciate that sentiment as much as I do one day. I hope I get to see mannerisms, facial expressions, personality traits of theirs that remind me of the best parts of my mom one day too. Kinslee's is already very obvious. She has my mom's beautiful blue eyes. From what I know of his personality now, I have a feeling Keaton will be strong-minded and stubborn just like she was. Kole's little hands have reminded me of my mom's since the first time I laid eyes on them the day he was born. Something about the shape of his fingers and his palms. They've always looked like hers to me. I can't wait to keep seeing the little things that make them unique but also give me glimpses of their maternal grandmother one day.

I've always felt the need to be strong, resilient, one that wipes away the tears as quickly as they fall. It was no different at twelve and it's no different now. Now that I've had time to reflect on my past, I know it's because I was forced to grow up at such a young age. Madeline and my dad needed me to be strong for them. I needed to be strong for myself. There was no other way I was going to get through what I went through for so many years.

My dad still says it, even now: "You've always been the strong one. I've never had to worry about you."

For most of my life, I wore that like a badge of honor—this silent strength I was praised for, the steady one, the one who didn't need saving. But the truth is, no one can hold it all together forever. Even the strongest structures crack under pressure. Looking back, I realize I wasn't holding strong— I was quietly unraveling. I was breaking in invisible ways, fractures forming in places no one could see. I just got really good at hiding the damage. I kept smiling. I kept showing up. I kept appearing whole. But inside, I was carrying a weight that kept growing heavier, pretending I was okay when I wasn't. I know now—I've been broken for a long time. I was just too busy being "the strong one" to admit it to myself.

Losing my mom made me realize how broken I was. I was forced to sit in sorrow, to look inside myself and realize how hurt I'd been for so long. I was so hurt, so broken, that I couldn't even comprehend a life of peace and content. I had no idea what it was like to not worry *constantly* over another human. It's exhausting. It really is.

I guess this book is my way of finally confessing the truth. Sharing with you the parts of my story that I've always tucked far away. The story that I've hidden because it makes me feel vulnerable and ashamed. The story that brings out my weaknesses through memories I still find hard to bear and emotions I still find hard to control. What I've finally realized is that these experiences in life, my story, have given me the strength others admire in me. For that, I am proud.

As I discussed in the beginning of this book, acceptance has been a difficult stage for me to process. Acceptance, for me, looks a lot like happiness in a life without my mom. Because to be able to really *feel* happiness, to feel joy, you can't also be sad, right? And I've absolutely felt happiness in many capacities over the course of life without her. Does that mean I'm no longer sad to have lost my mom? Does it make me a bad person to finally be able to see the areas of my life, my well-being, my mental health that improved from her loss?

I don't have these answers. I just want anyone else reading this who may be able to relate to any of my story, to any of these feelings to know that you're not alone. That it's okay to be selfish, to think selfishly, to act selfishly to get yourself through your grieving process. For me, when my mom passed away, the only memories I was flooded with were the good ones. That was okay at first. I wanted to remember all the best things about her, all of the best memories we made together. Selective memory is the technical term for it. The tendency to only remember certain aspects of a situation while forgetting others. It's viewed as a defense mechanism in grief and can potentially hinder the grieving process. For many years, those rose-tinted glasses were unknowingly delaying my healing. The more I focused on everything I missed about her, the more the gaping hole she left grew. It wasn't until I stopped filtering out the negative aspects that I truly began to heal. As sad as it is to admit this was my door to healing, there is beauty in accepting the importance of remembering the whole picture. The loss I was grieving for so long was the loss of my mom on her good days. I'd completely filtered out the aspects of her, the mom I had on bad days, that caused years of distress and heartbreak in our lives. I had to learn how to prioritize those negative memories, to intentionally draw attention to them in moments of intense sadness, to even begin to learn how to look on the bright side again.

There's no denying the hole I'll always feel in my heart and in my life without her. It doesn't feel natural to live a life without a mom because it *isn't* natural. The reality is, she was supposed to be here.

She was supposed to meet my husband, to tell me she knew it in her heart he was the one for me. She was supposed to be here to help me pick out my wedding dress, to watch me walk down the aisle. She was supposed to be here to hold her first granddaughter in the hospital room, to answer my call in the middle of the night when she had her first fever and I didn't know what to do. She was supposed to be the one to make cupcakes to reveal the gender of our twins, to tell me how proud she was of me on the day they were born. She was supposed to give me advice as I prepared for my first big management interview, to help me pick out what to wear. She was supposed to be here to see her grandchildren grow up, to remind me that the days are long but the years are fast. I'm reminded every single day of this life that she should be here.

The true healing came in remembering that I was hurting long before she was gone. That hurt was different though, it was inflicted by her *living.* The amount of stress, heartbreak, disappointment, dread, defeat, sadness I endured every day of my life for so many years—while she was still here and *because of her*—are truths I had to accept. When I could finally shift my perspective and recognize the sense of relief I felt to no longer have all of "those things" weighing on me constantly, I could finally take a step forward. I was ready to see the sun shine again.

What I've learned over time is that everything I've felt and still feel are totally normal responses to the loss I've endured. It's called grief. For so long, I looked at my tendencies to shut down and push away as a form of weakness. As if only the strongest are capable of opening up and letting people in. But that's just not who I am. That's not how I cope with sadness. That's not how I grieve from loss.

What I've learned is that acceptance isn't moving on. It's not accepting life without my mom. It's not accepting that she's never coming back. For me, acceptance is finally being okay with welcoming happiness back into my life. Knowing that I can still miss her immensely and want her here but also knowing that it's okay to look on the bright side of the very unfortunate outcome. The two feelings—happiness *and* sadness- can unapologetically coexist. Acceptance is taking a step forward, without her, knowing she'll never be forgotten. Acceptance is recognizing the strength it takes to be able to get to this point and being proud of how far you've come.

Acceptance, for me, was realizing that the house that broke me was actually the house that built me all along.

Made in the USA
Columbia, SC
20 May 2025

58092150R00169